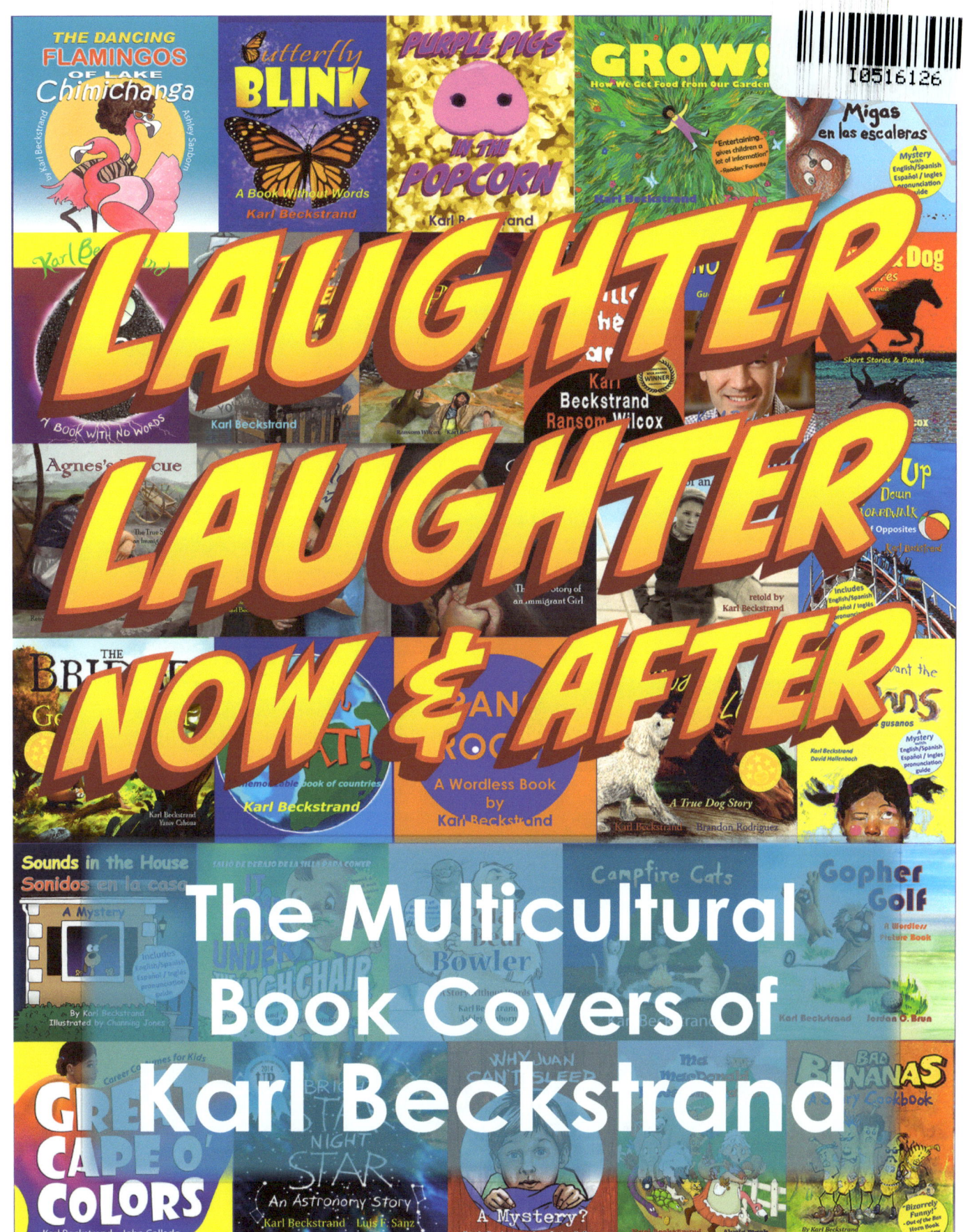

Laughter, Laughter—Now & After
The Multicultural Book Covers of Karl Beckstrand
(See if you catch three narratives reading each title in order:)

Premio Publishing & Gozo Books, Midvale, UT, USA
Library of Congress Control Number: 2024936438
ISBN: **978-1951599232** (ebook: 979-8224478552)

Text & Illustration Copyright © 2024 Karl Beckstrand
For my amazing artists/illustrators!

COUNT THE CIRCLES!

Great Cape o' Colors – Capa de colores (English-Spanish with pronunciation guide) →
"Bright illustrations.… excellent for teachers." – Maritza Mejia, writer/educator

"This is a magic cape!" "Ésta es una capa mágica". Explore daring jobs and count the cultures—has full text and pronunciation guide in both Spanish and English (for emergent readers ages 3 years and up, Pre-K – 6th grade, ESL/ELL/EFL, easy to read & level 1 ESOL/ESE).

Discover online adventure secrets and learn some color theory with Hispanic and black superhero characters. Dress up! Make a game of pretending to be the different characters (try on costumes). Available in single language—also a coloring book! 100 dyslexic-friendly words, 28 pages, 8.5"x8.5"; hard ISBN: 978-1732069619, soft: 978-0692220986, ebook ISBN: 978-1370809332, Spanish-only: 978-1986734066, coloring book ISBN: 978-1719025935

All rights reserved: This book, or parts thereof, may not be reproduced or shared in any form—except by reviewer, who may quote brief passages or sample illustrations in a printed, online, or broadcast review—without prior written permission from the publisher.
Derechos reservados. Queda prohibida la reproducción o transmisión de parte alguna de esta obra, sin permiso escrito del publicador.

ORDER direct or via major distributors.

FREE multicultural ebooks, lesson plans, exclusive bundles & online SECRETS gratis:
PremioPublishing.com

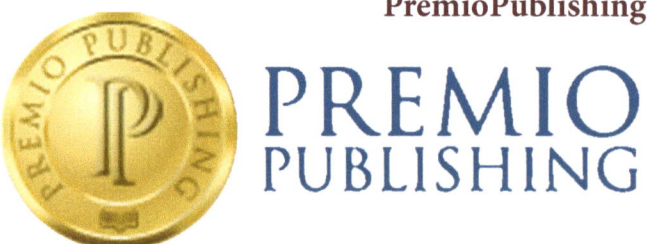

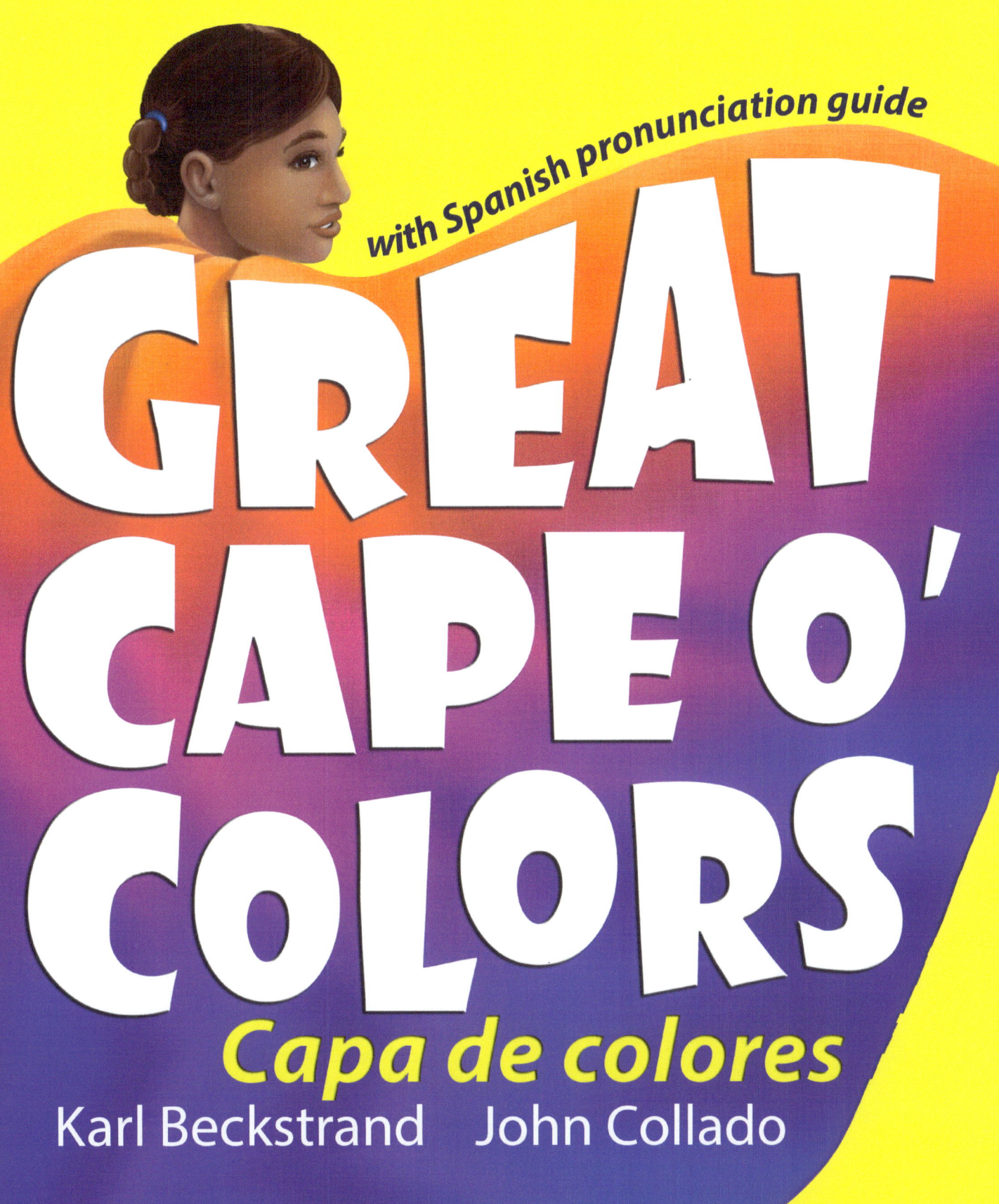

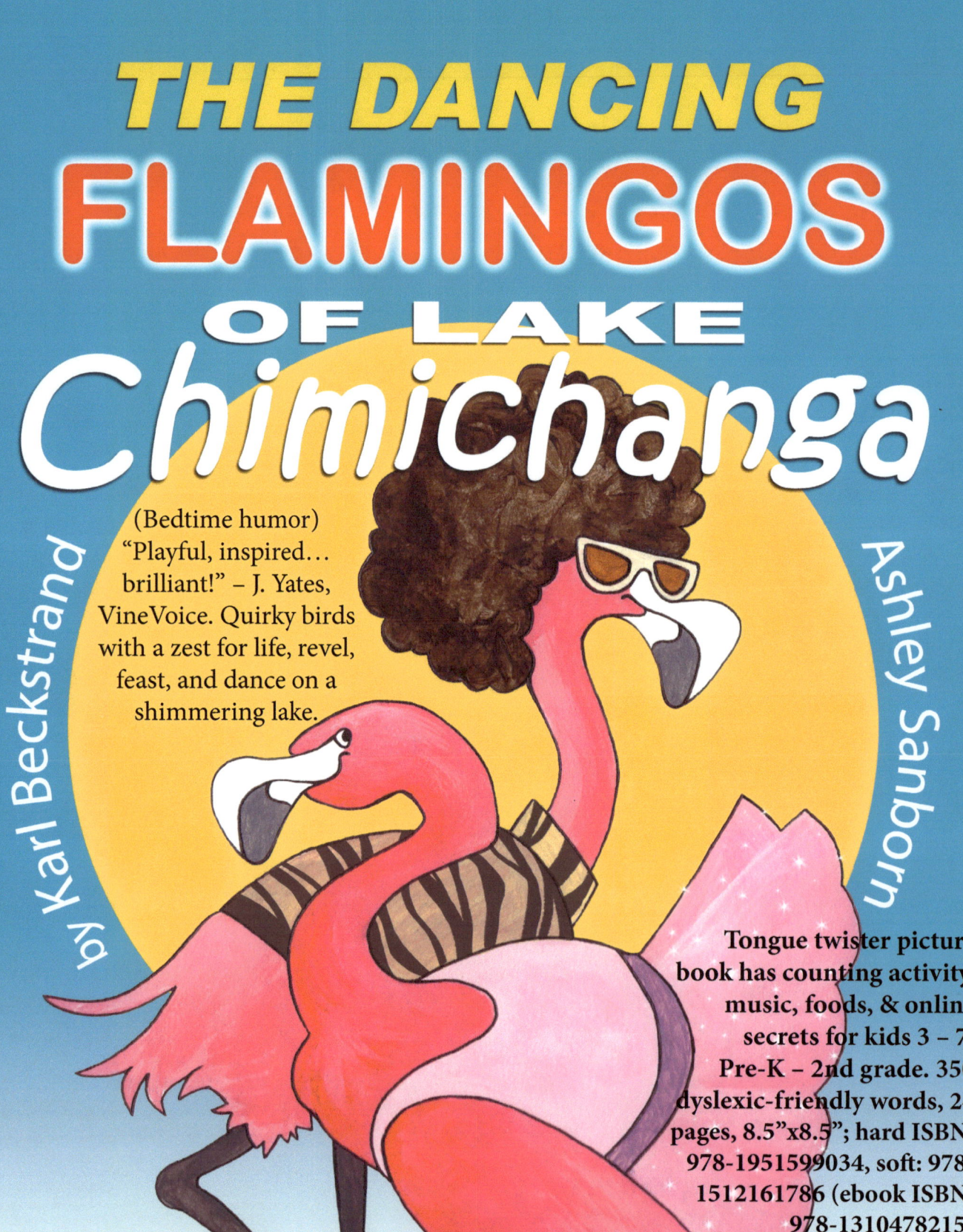

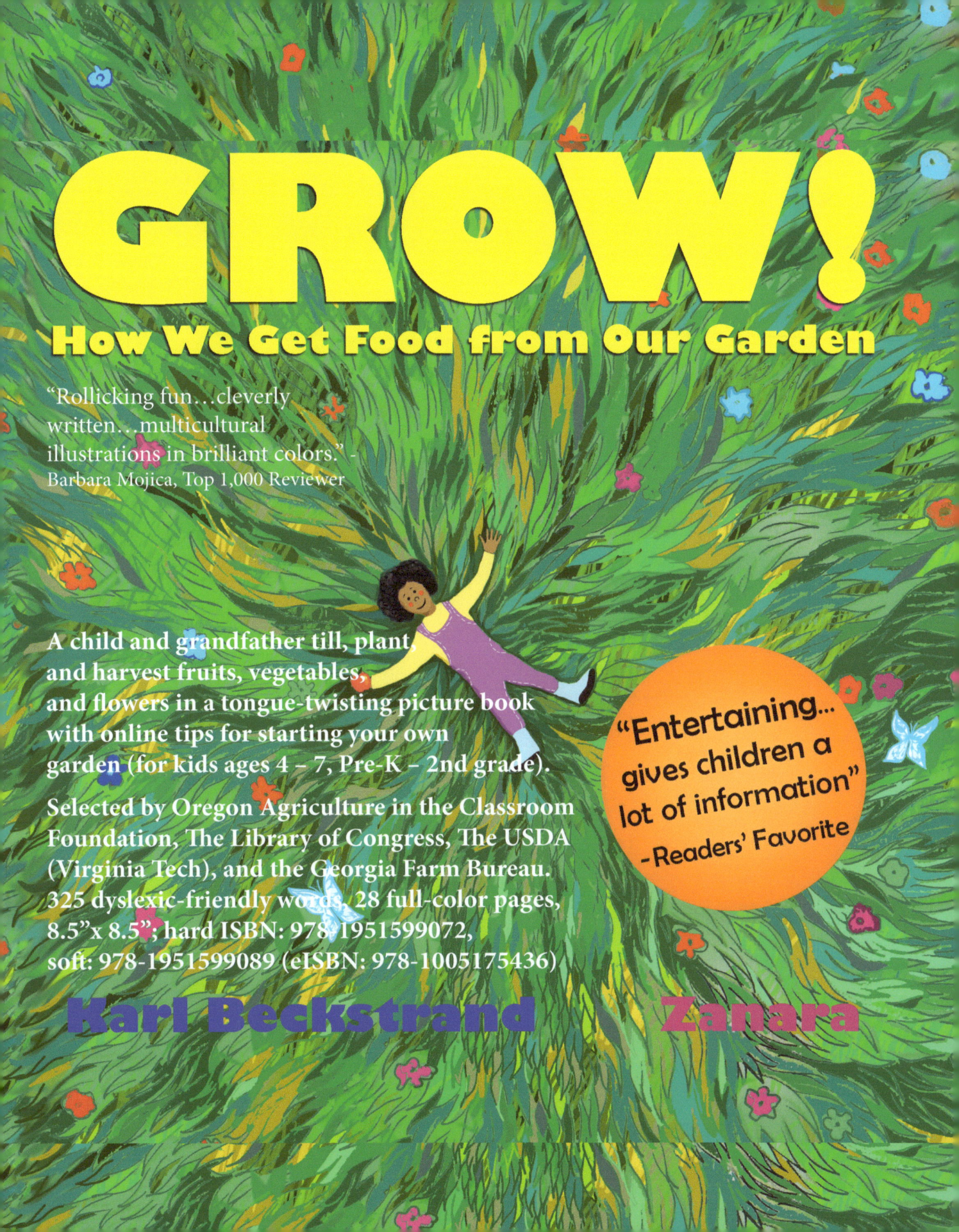

BAD BANANAS
A Story Cookbook

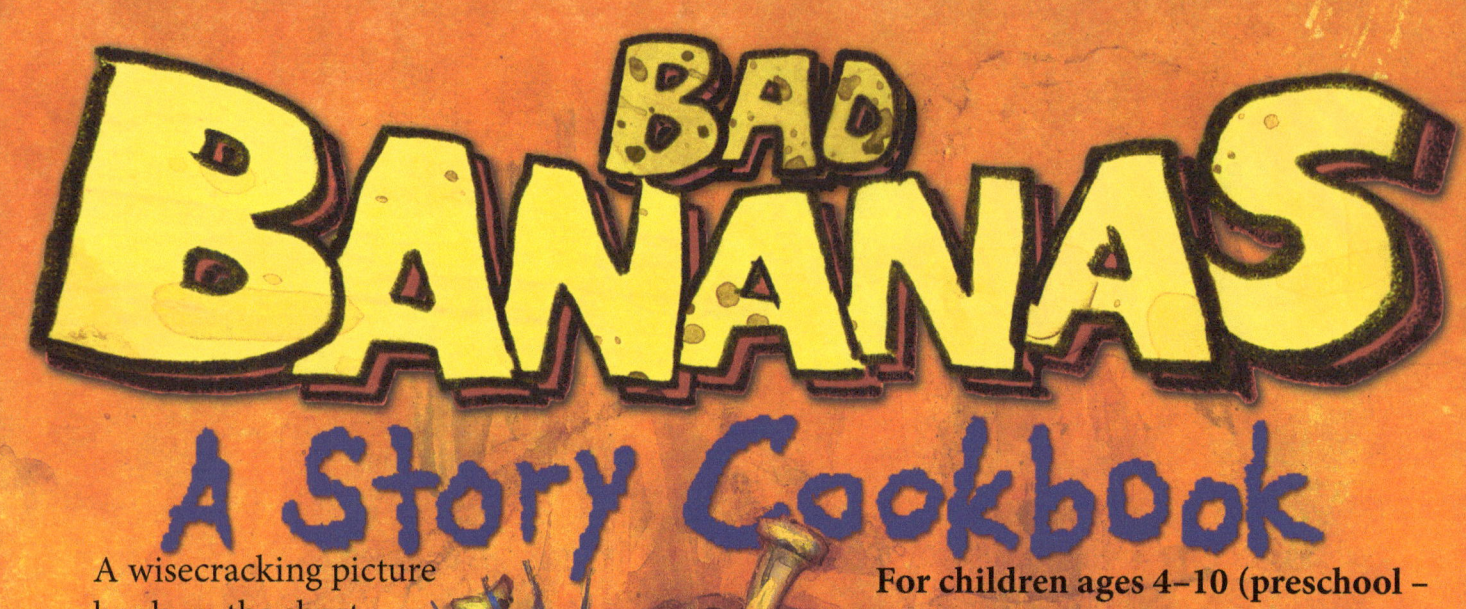

A wisecracking picture book on the short (shelf) life of a bunch of bruisers with seven easy, low-sugar recipes. The perfect family activity: tasty, funny, hands-on fun.

For children ages 4–10 (preschool – 5th grade); 320 words (before recipes), 24 full-color illustrations; black and Hispanic characters; 8"x10"; hard ISBN: 978-0977606542, soft ISBN: 978-0977606511 (ebook: 978-1452415598)

"Bizarrely Funny!" - Out of the Box Horn Book blog review

By Karl Beckstrand
Illustrated by Jeff Faerber

Kids tell the story! Watch as a hermit crab and a tortoise find and plant a mysterious seed. See what grows and discover online secrets. Kids cement vocabulary as they describe the events (for beginner readers ages 1 – 6, Pre-K – 1st grade, Sept. 2024). 24 full-color illustrations; 8.5" x 8.5"; hard ISBN: 978-1951599249, soft ISBN: 978-1951599256

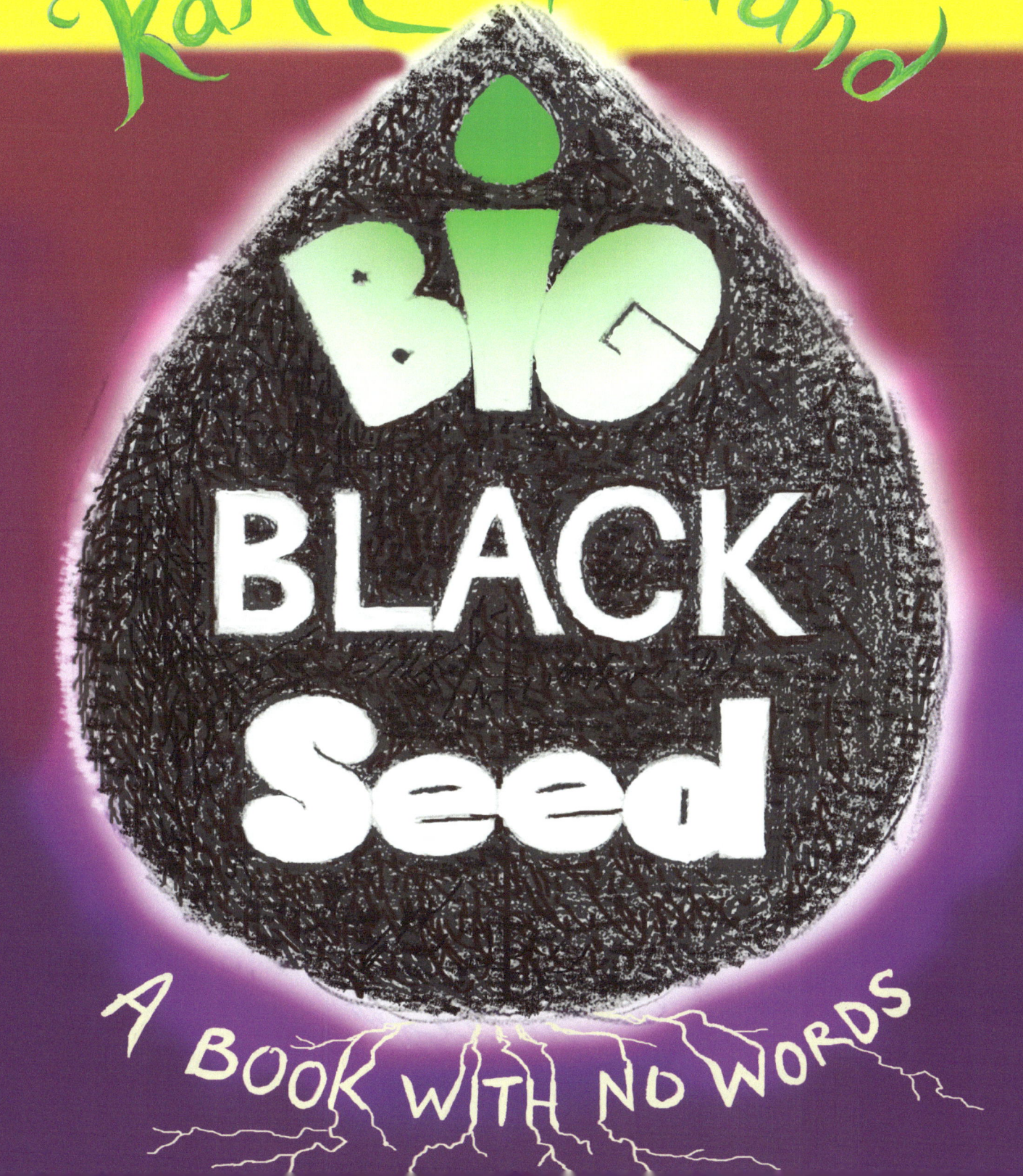

"Brilliant…teaching at the same time. Fantastic book." – Amanda Williams, U.K. A mysterious visitor brings intrigue and humor to a biracial family. A picture book of prepositions, monsters, and heroes—with finding/counting activity, language pronunciation guide, and online SECRETS

SALIÓ DE DEBAJO DE LA SILLA PARA COMER

IT CAME FROM UNDER THE HIGH CHAIR

A MYSTERY

Spanish & English with pronunciation guide

Karl Beckstrand

Jeremy Higginbotham

For kids ages 4+, Pre-K – 7th grade. 36 full-color pages, 8.5"x8.5", 800 words in dyslexic-friendly type (double for bilingual); also available in single language, hard ISBN: 978-1732069664, soft: 978-0692220993, eISBN: 978-0463454855, Spanish-only: 978-1076006516

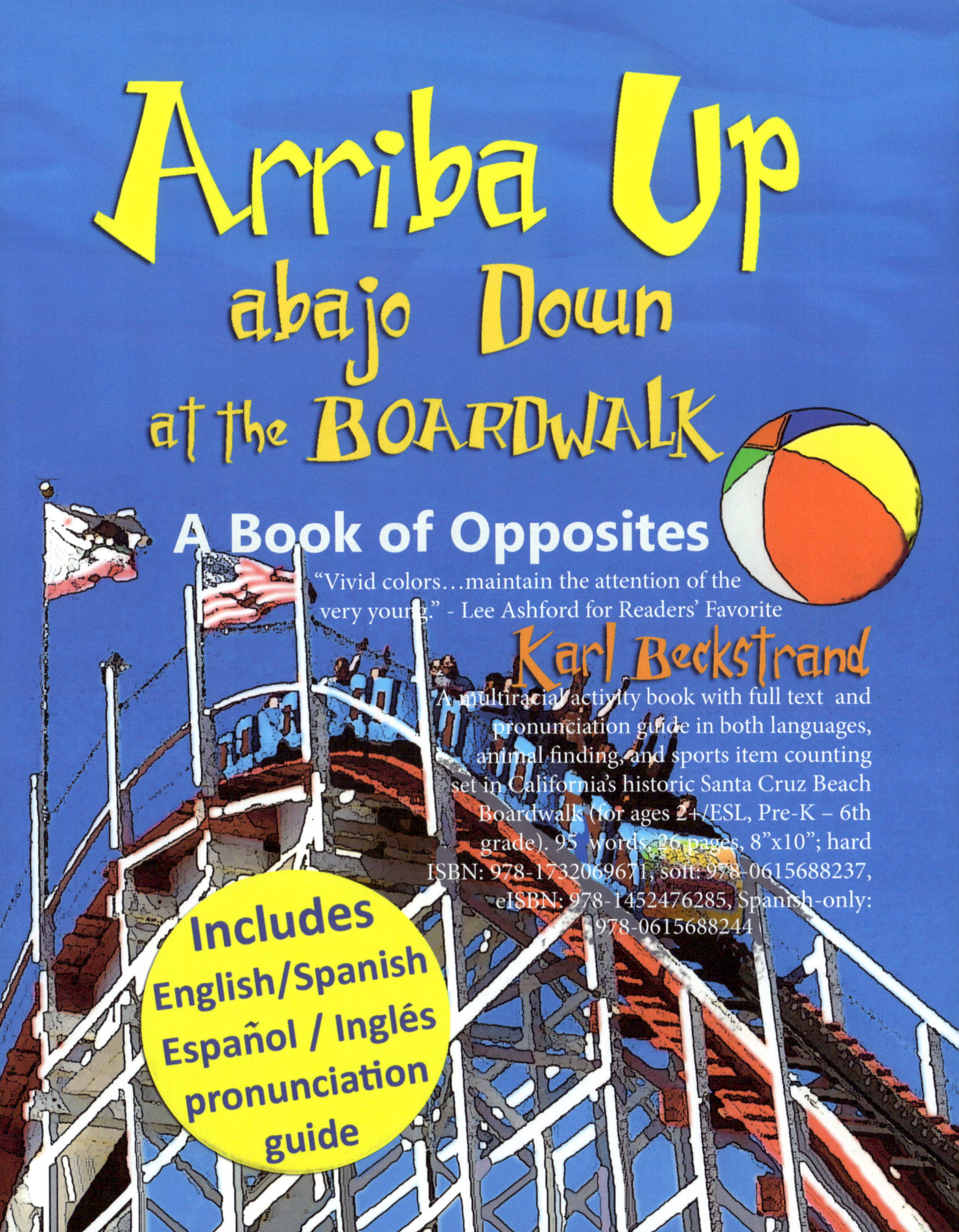

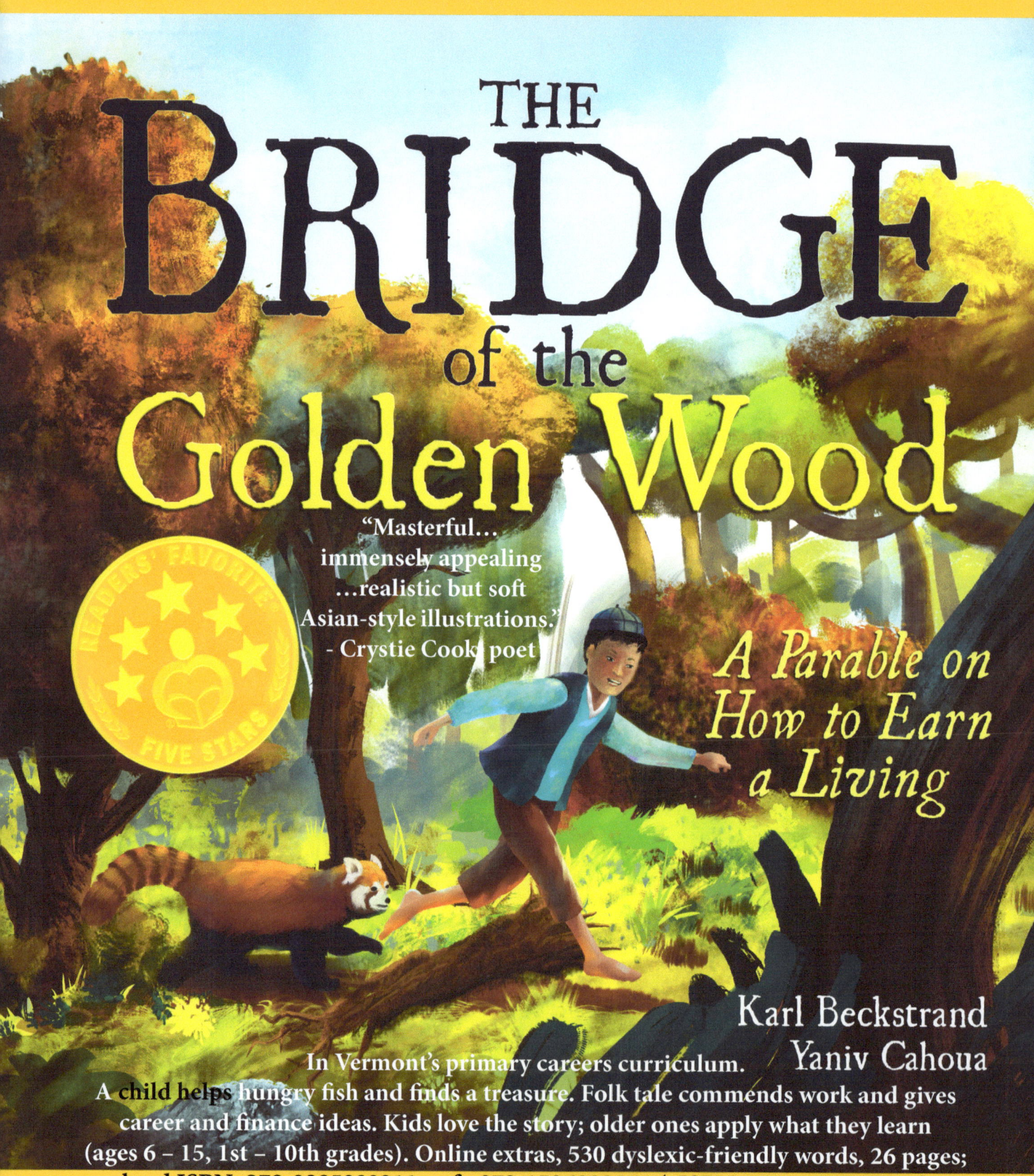

THE BRIDGE of the Golden Wood

"Masterful… immensely appealing …realistic but soft Asian-style illustrations."
- Crystie Cook, poet

A Parable on How to Earn a Living

Karl Beckstrand
Yaniv Cahoua

In Vermont's primary careers curriculum. A child helps hungry fish and finds a treasure. Folk tale commends work and gives career and finance ideas. Kids love the story; older ones apply what they learn (ages 6 – 15, 1st – 10th grades). Online extras, 530 dyslexic-friendly words, 26 pages; hard ISBN: 978-0985398811, soft: 978-1536889864 (eISBN: 978-1370287222)

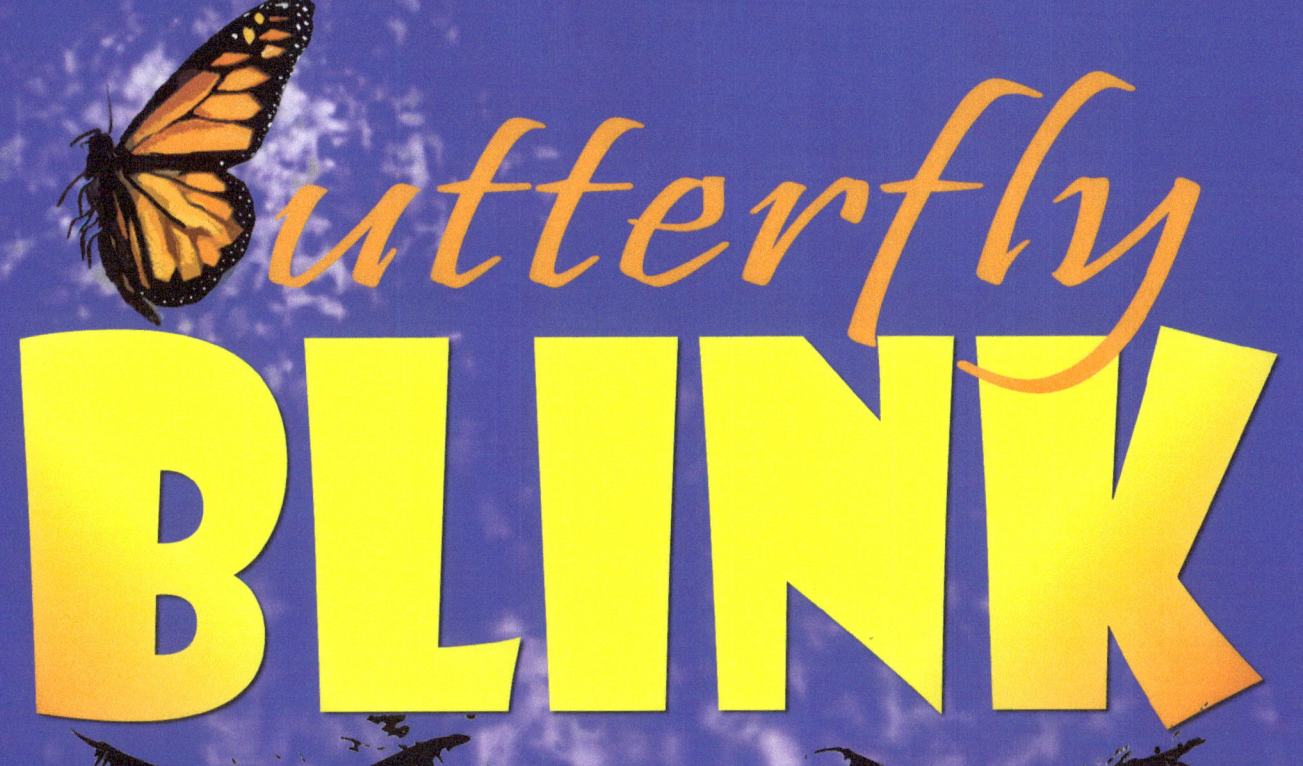

Butterfly BLINK

(STEM) "Entranced me…fascinating concept…luscious colors…stunning illustrations." - Jean B. Yates, Vine Voice Reviewer. Winner: Promoting Picture Books' Art Cover Contest. Kids (2 – 6, Pre-K – 1st grade) cement vocabulary as they tell/write the story. Blink—and the butterflies multiply. Hidden picture, insect habitat conservation info, online secrets, and characters of color; 24 full-color pages (8"x10"); hard ISBN: 978-1951599010, soft: 978-0692648599 (ebook ISBN: 978-1311095978)

A Book Without Words

Karl Beckstrand

WHY JUAN CAN'T SLEEP

"Crosses cultural boundaries... Lovely exploration... fabulously rich and evocative of the artistry of Shel Silverstein."
– M. Condon, Unite for Literacy.

(Bedtime humor) "Crazy day— of work and play—worn-out Juan 'Must sleep!' Tonight he'll dream of dragons…" Discover animals, Spanglish, and parts of speech (for ages 4 - 7, Pre-K –3rd grade). 8"x10", 32 pages, 290 words; hard ISBN: 978-1951599041, soft: 978-0615692296 (eISBN: 978-13012 87598)

A Mystery?

Karl Beckstrand   Luis F. Sanz

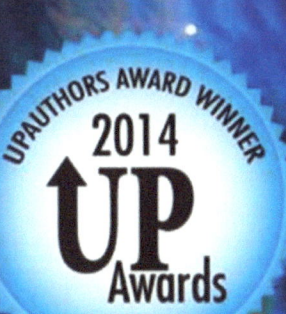

"Guides readers into a world that is eye-opening and page-turning!" - UP Authors. Join a Native American child exploring the mysteries of the universe. Discover the magic of moons, meteors, constellations, and galaxies. STEM picture book with online secrets and glossary for kids 4 – 9 (Pre-K – 4th grade). 8.5"x8.5", 400 words, 30 pages; hard ISBN: 978-0985398880, soft: 978-0615856155 (eISBN: 978-1310128097)

BRIGHT STAR NIGHT STAR

An Astronomy Story

Karl Beckstrand **Luis F. Sanz**

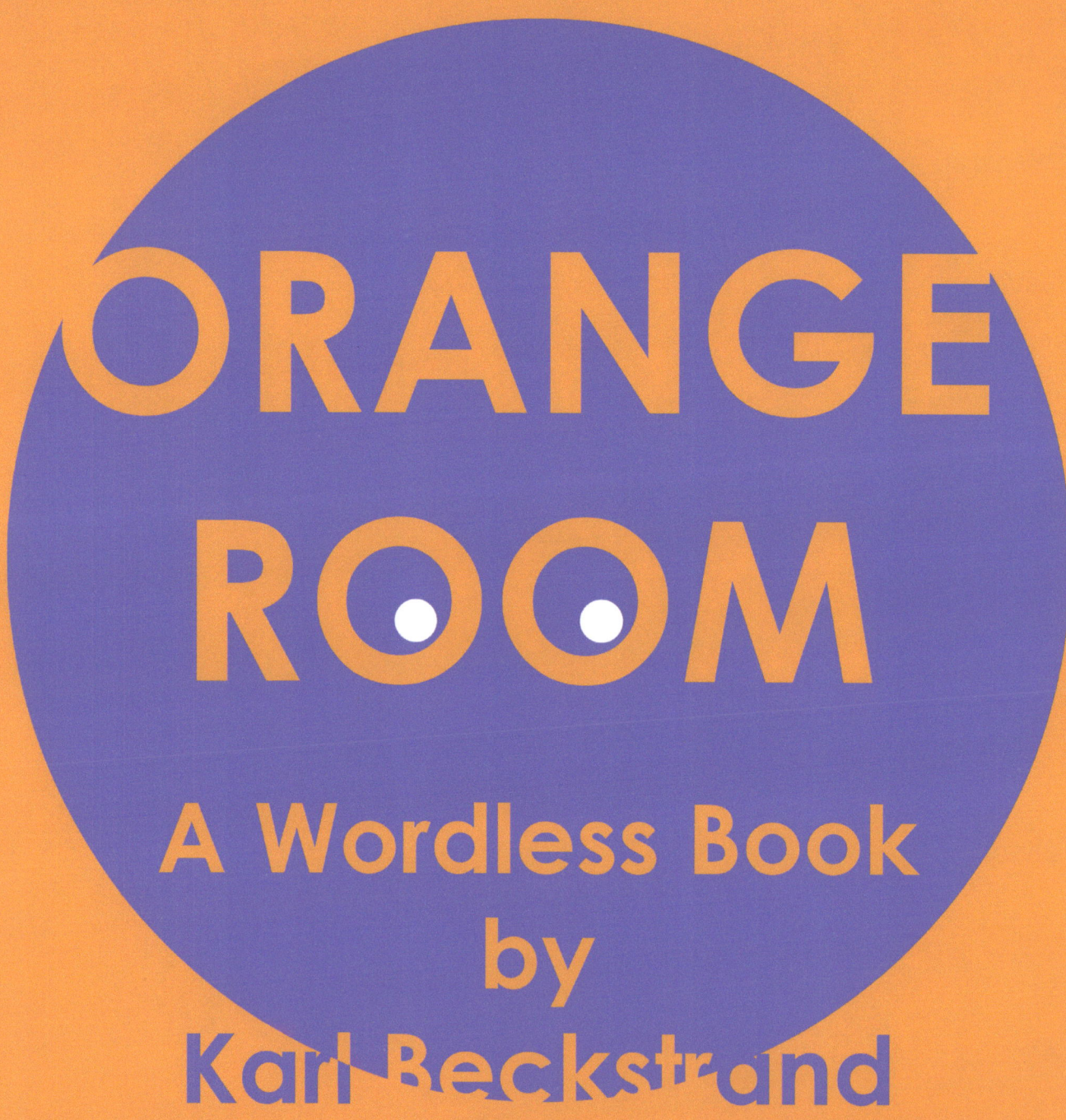

(Concepts) A Menagerie of fruits, flowers, minerals, and mammals —ALL orange!
For kids ages 3 – 6, Pre-K – 1st grade; 28 pages, 8.5"x8.5"; ISBN: 978-1951599331.
PRE-ORDER: 2025 release

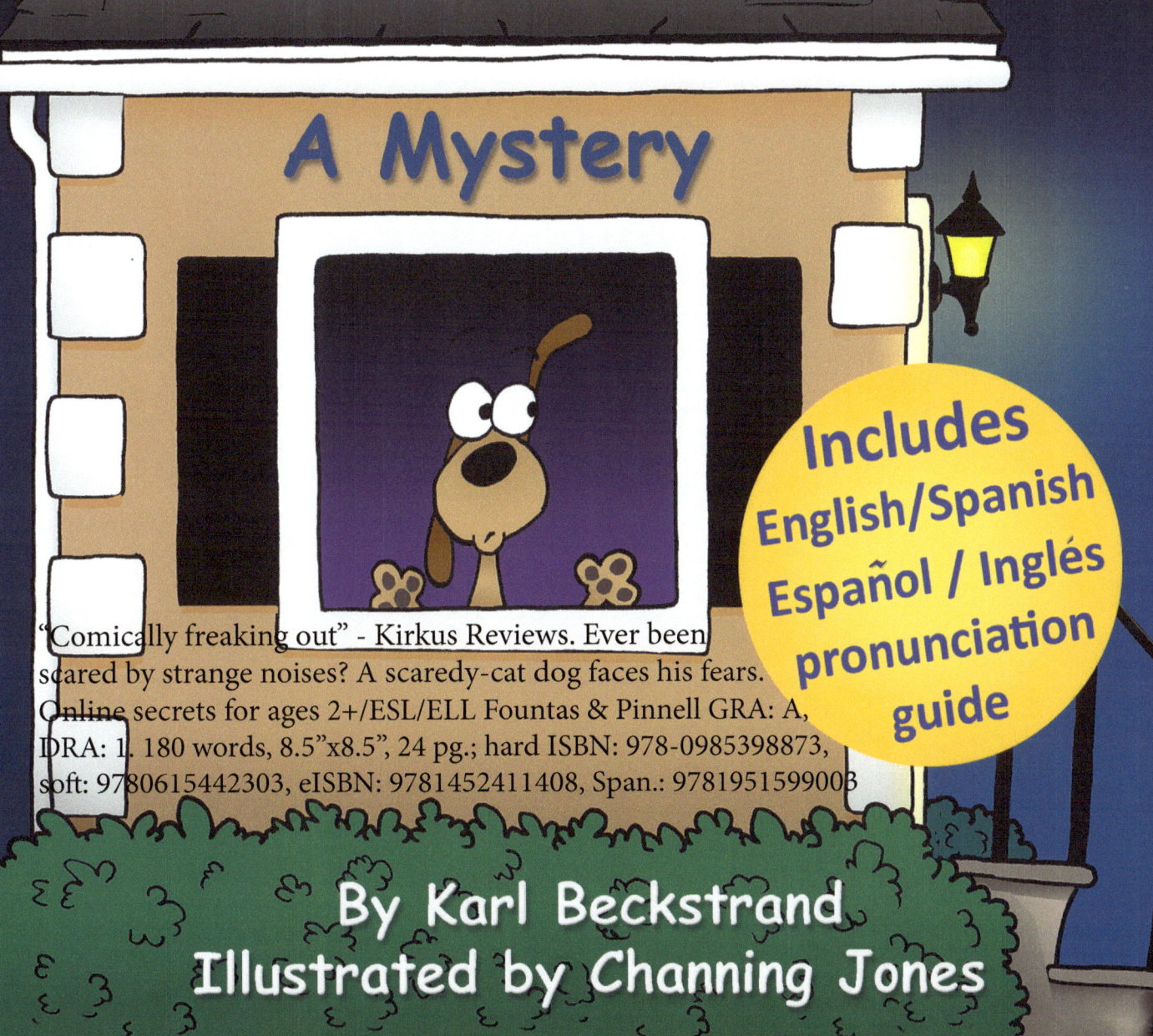

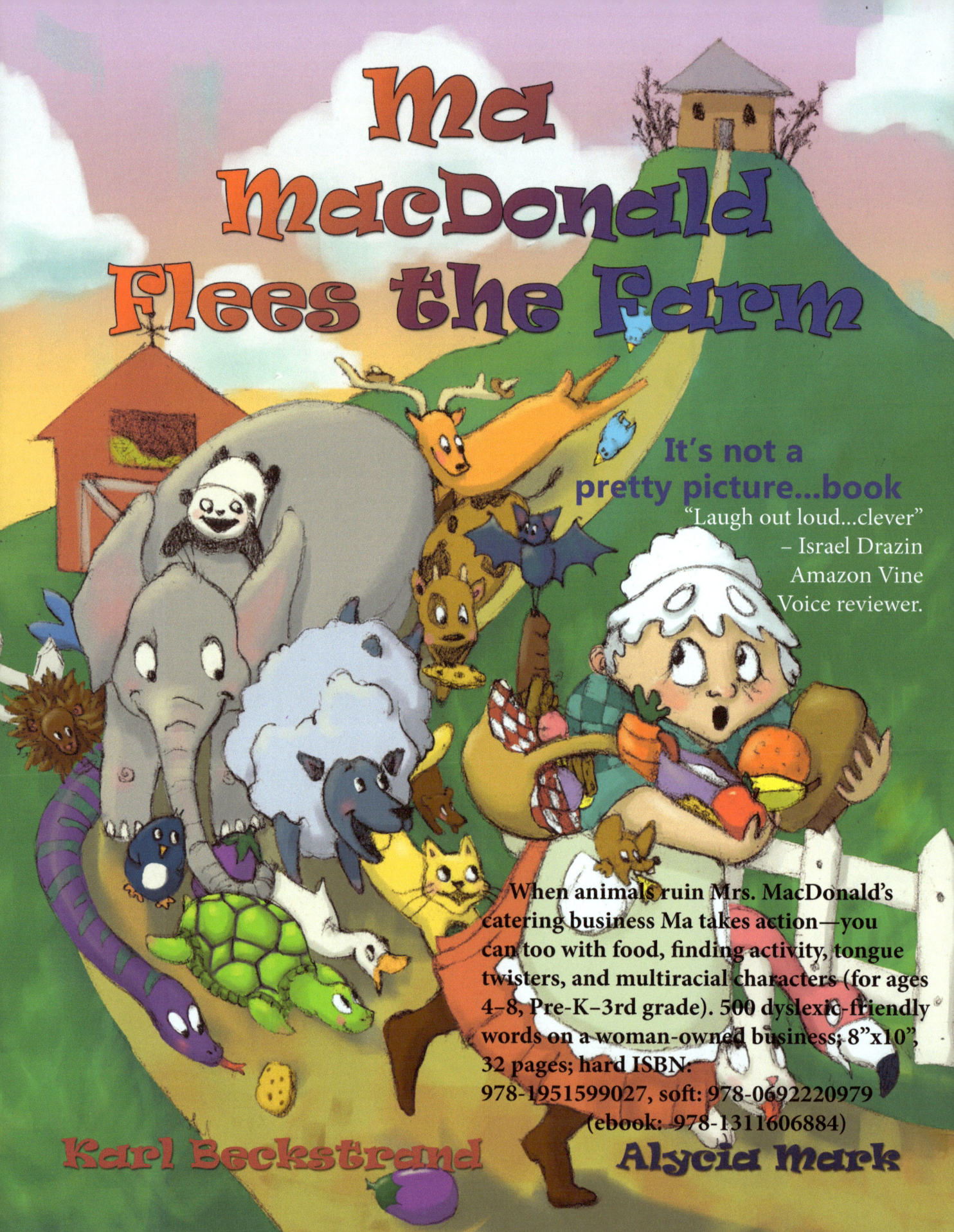

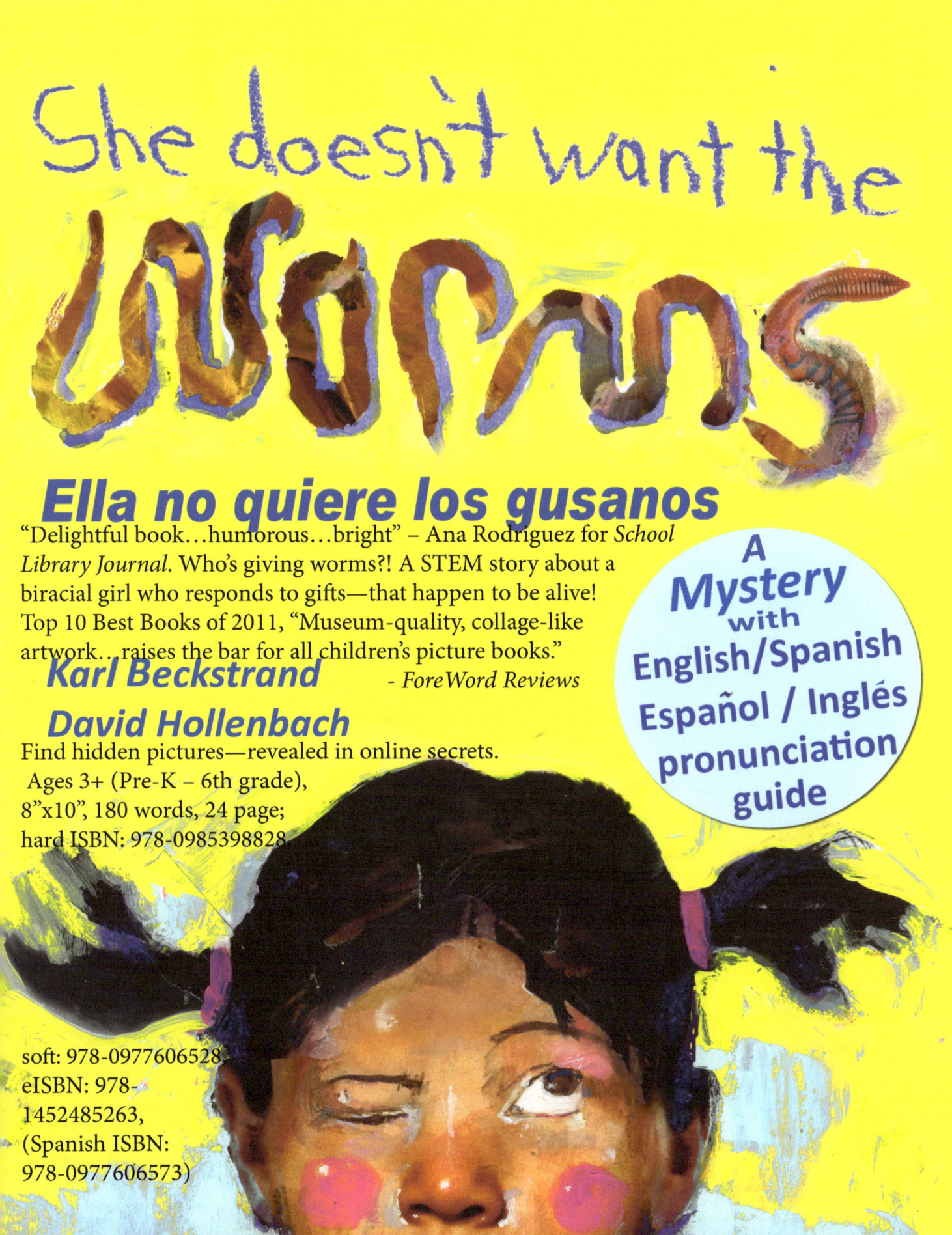

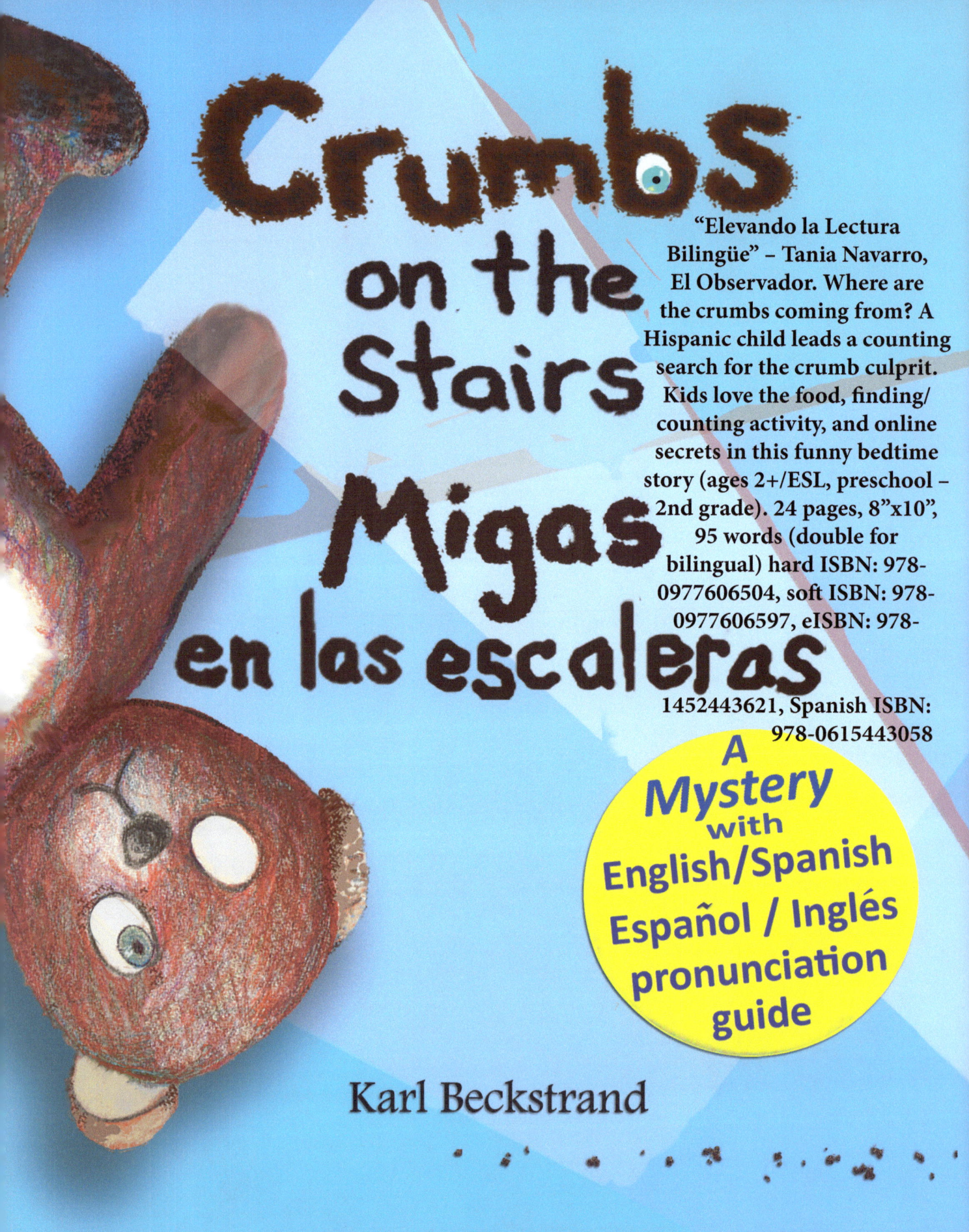

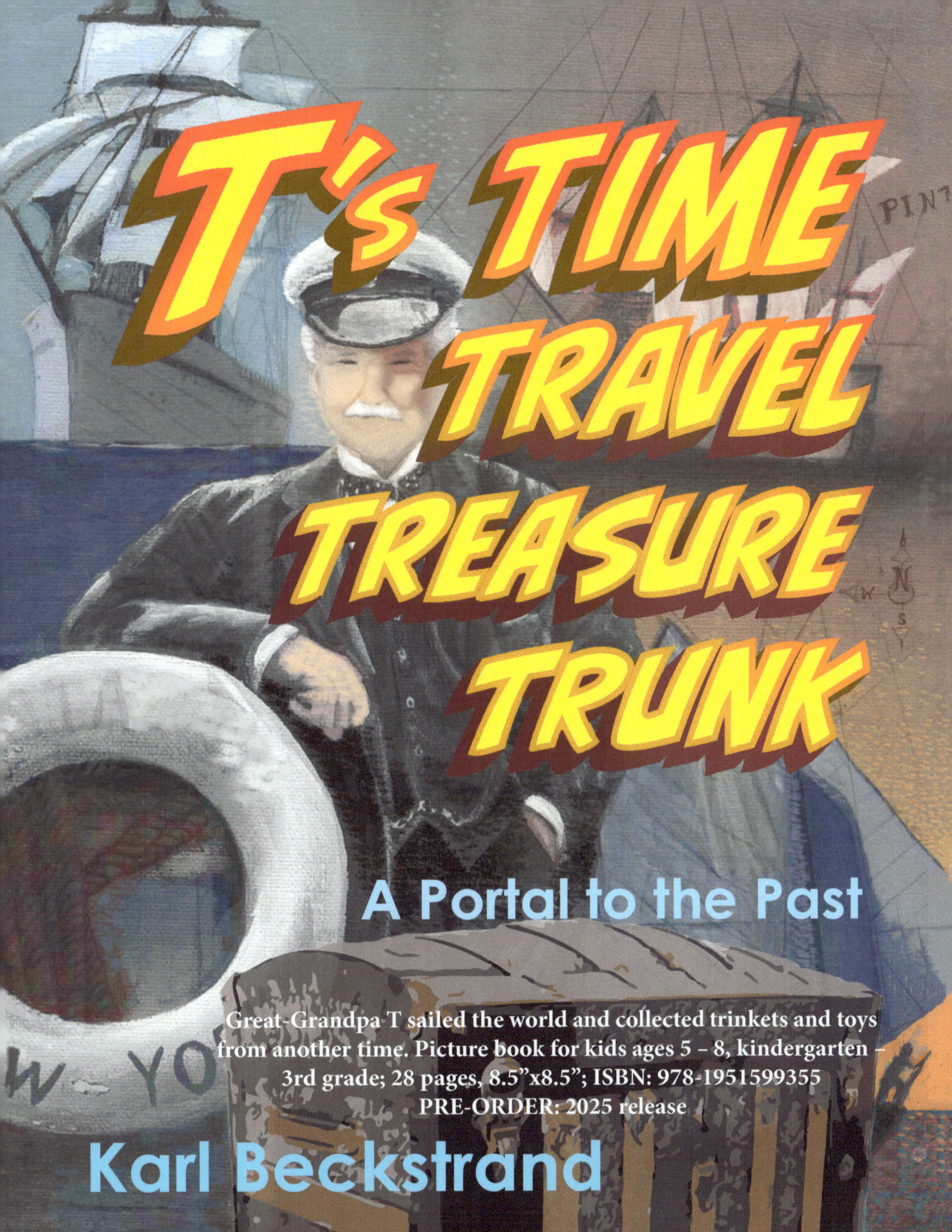

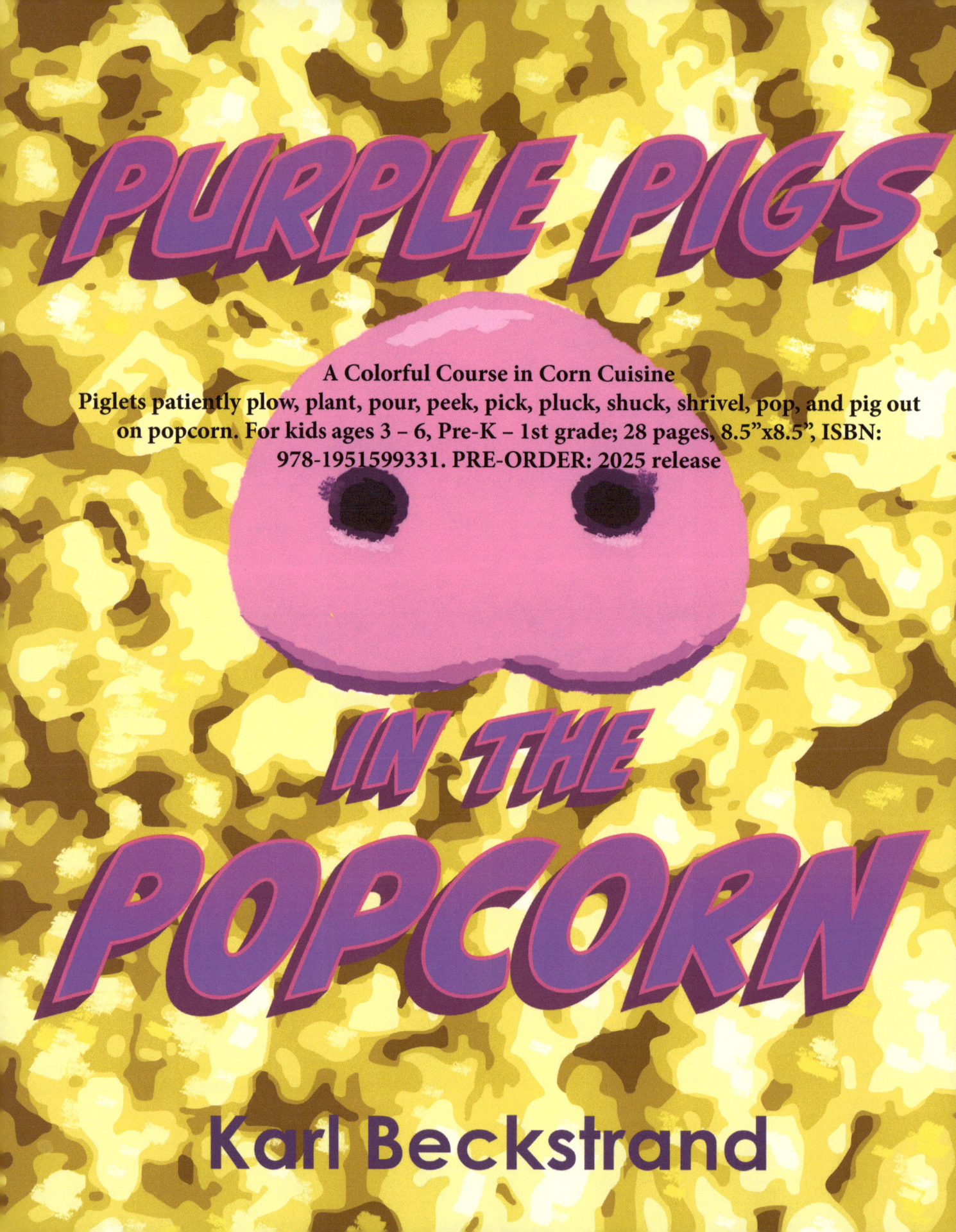

Horse & Dog
Adventures
in Early California

"Simple language and homespun charm" – Barbara Mojica, Top 1,000 Reviewer. Ransom Wilcox's adventures in the back country of Northern California show his love of animals and nature (for ages 9+, middle grade). Edited by Karl Beckstrand. 42 pages, 5.25" x 8", 8,000 words; soft ISBN: 978-0615856162, ebook ISBN: 978-1301904747

Short Stories & Poems

Ransom A. Wilcox

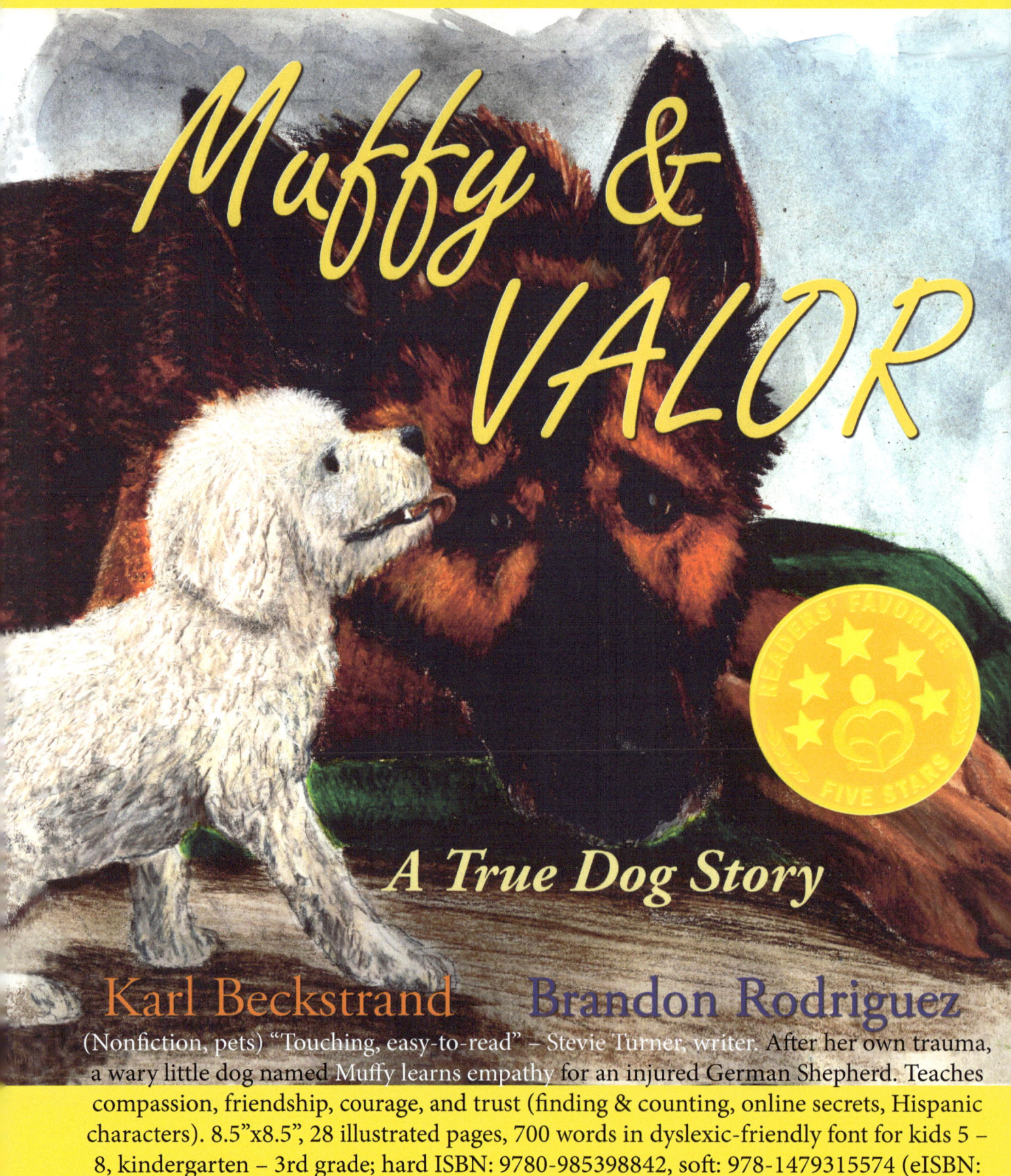

Muffy & VALOR

A True Dog Story

Karl Beckstrand   Brandon Rodriguez

(Nonfiction, pets) "Touching, easy-to-read" – Stevie Turner, writer. After her own trauma, a wary little dog named Muffy learns empathy for an injured German Shepherd. Teaches compassion, friendship, courage, and trust (finding & counting, online secrets, Hispanic characters). 8.5"x8.5", 28 illustrated pages, 700 words in dyslexic-friendly font for kids 5 – 8, kindergarten – 3rd grade; hard ISBN: 9780-985398842, soft: 978-1479315574 (eISBN: 978-1370601592)

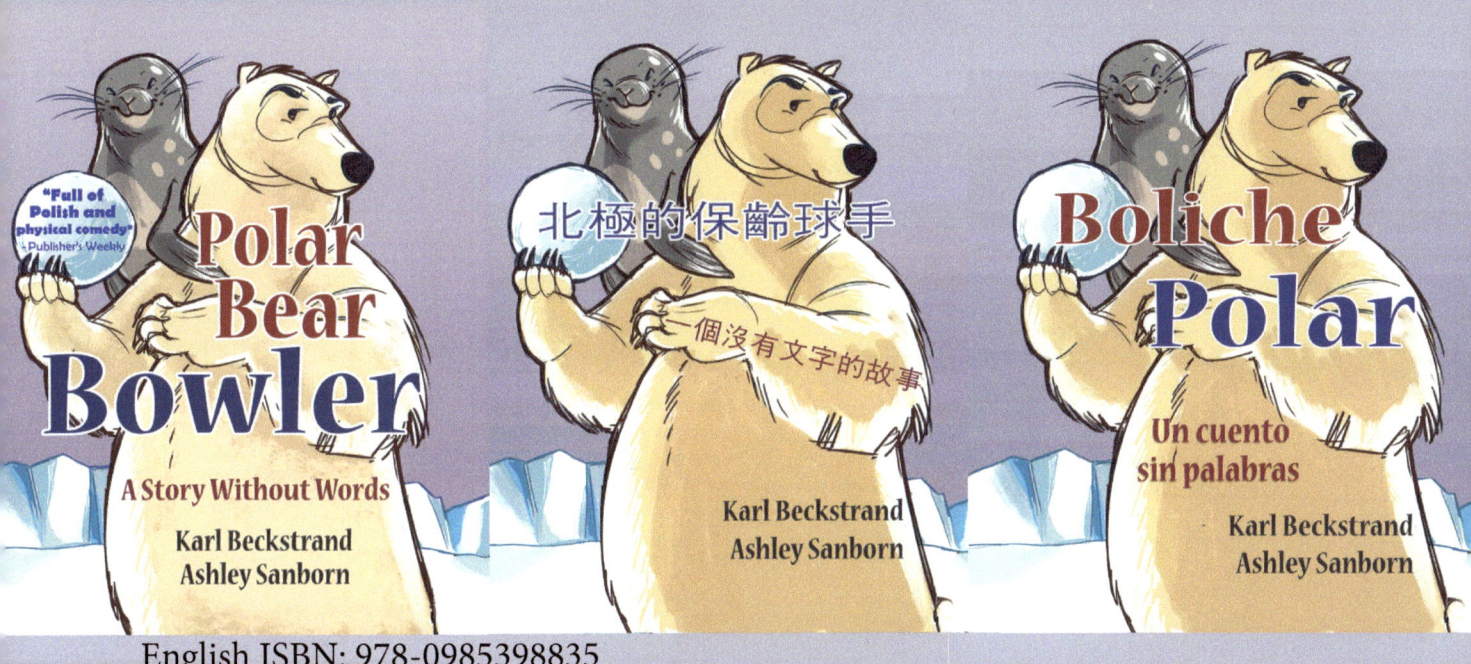

English ISBN: 978-0985398835

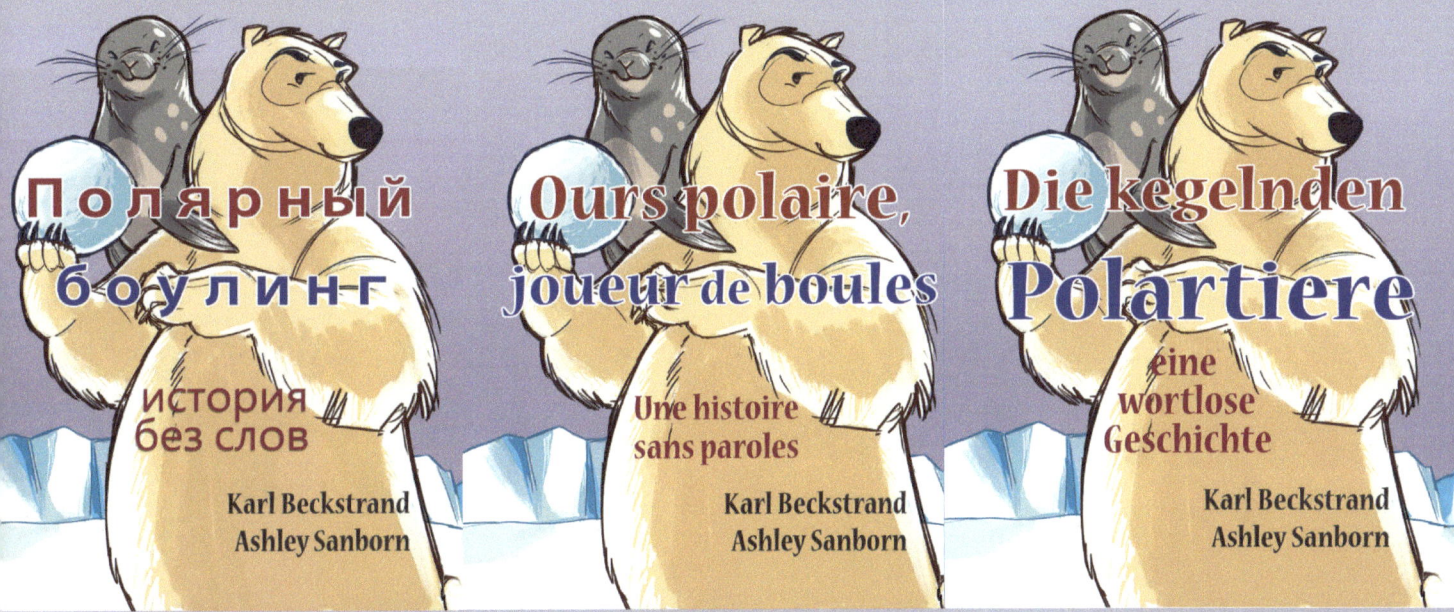

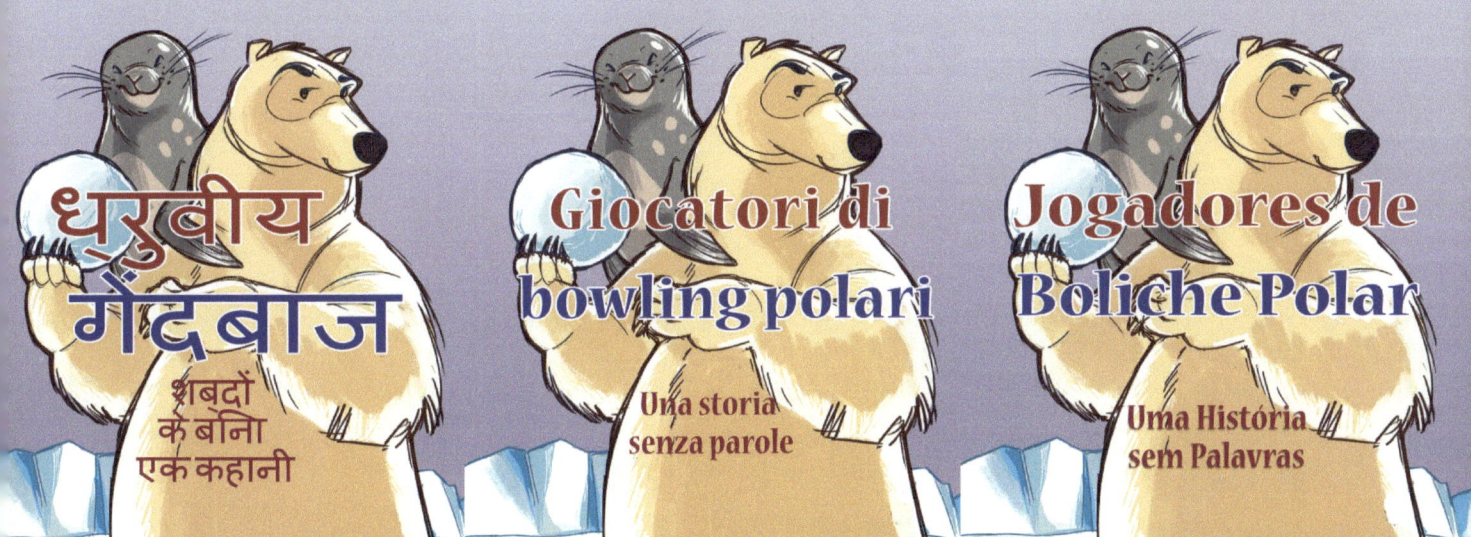

Campfire Cats

Feline Fun in the Forest. Doubtful Scouts swap stories and smores, sing, stalk, star gaze, and snooze. For kids ages 4 – 7, Pre-K – 2nd grade; 28 pages, 8.5"x8.5"; ISBN: 978-1951599362. PRE-ORDER: 2025 release

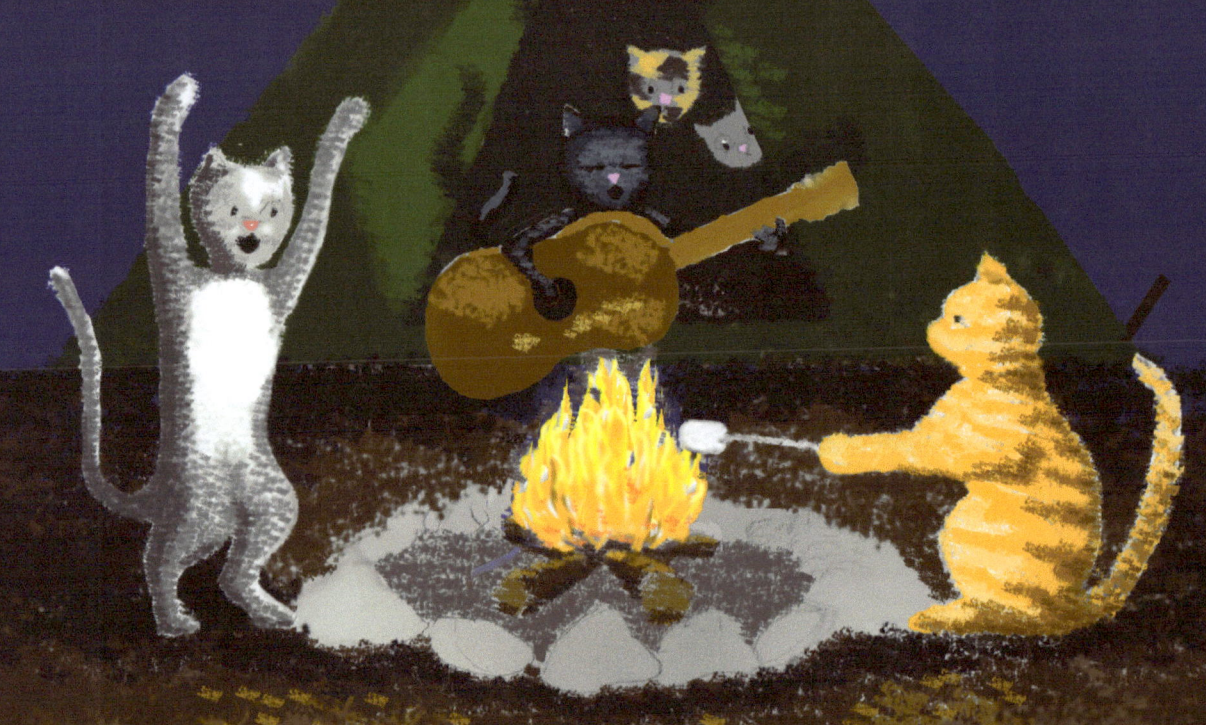

Karl Beckstrand

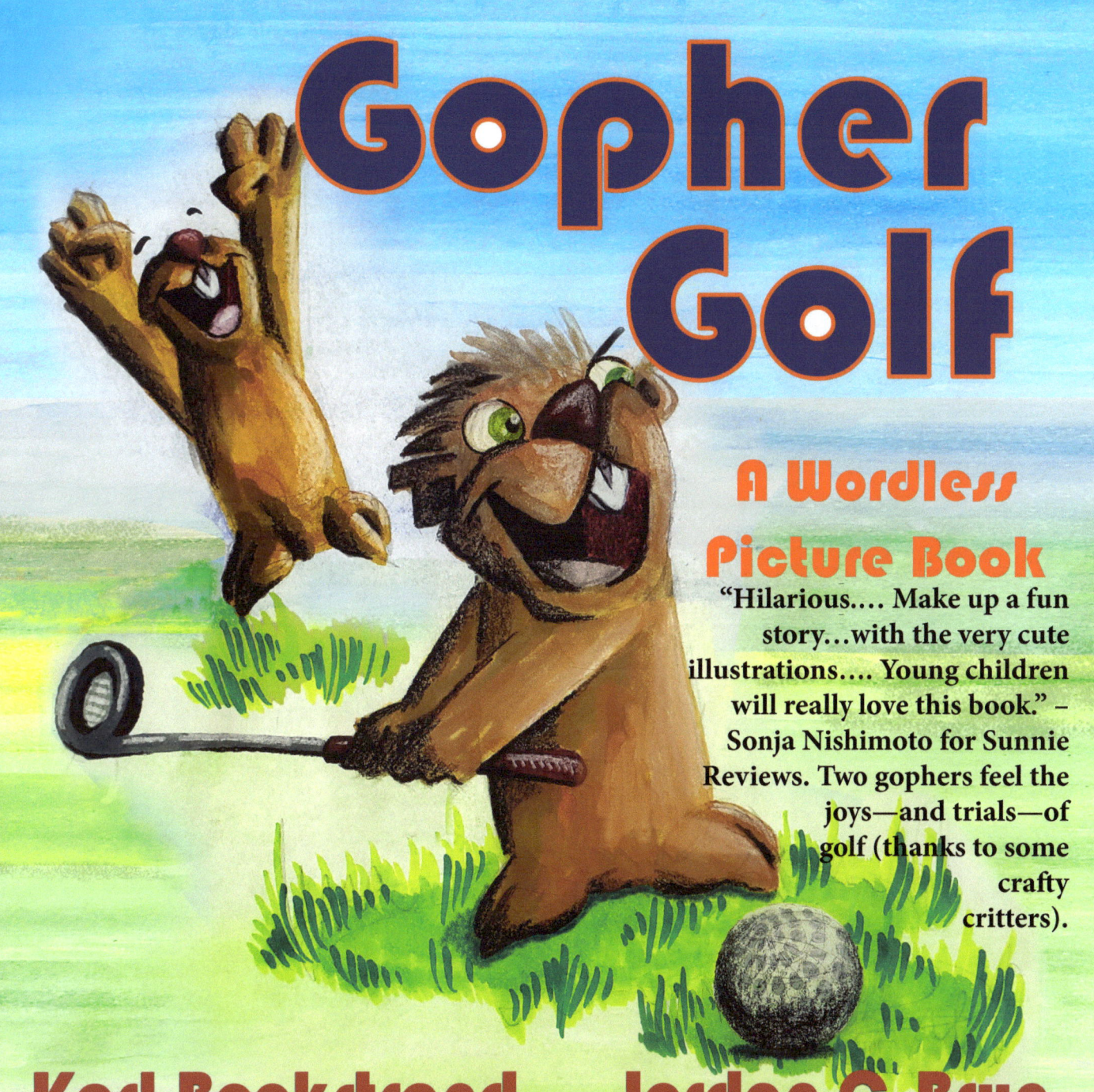

Gopher Golf

A Wordless Picture Book

"Hilarious.... Make up a fun story...with the very cute illustrations.... Young children will really love this book." – Sonja Nishimoto for Sunnie Reviews. Two gophers feel the joys—and trials—of golf (thanks to some crafty critters).

Karl Beckstrand   Jordan C. Brun

Write the story, find/name the animals, see online secrets, and cement vocabulary with this book for ages 2 – 6, Pre-K – 1st grade (ESL, Fountas & Pinnell GRA: A, DRA: 1). Low stimulation for autistic children; 30 pages, 8.5"x8.5"; hard ISBN: 978-1951599096, soft: 978-1951599102 (eISBN: 978-1005586782)

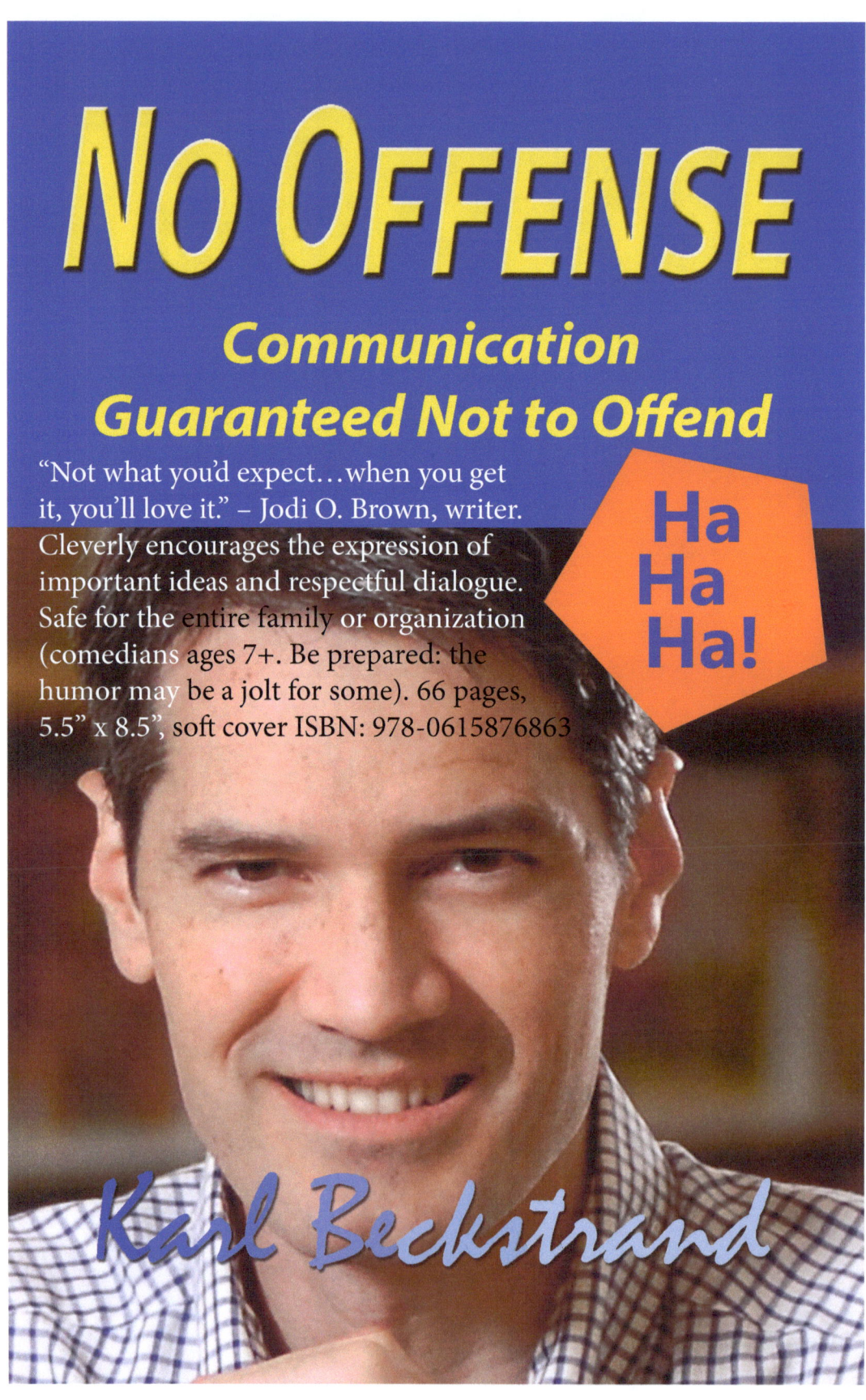

The End
Sort of...

Young American Immigrants (illustrated biography series)

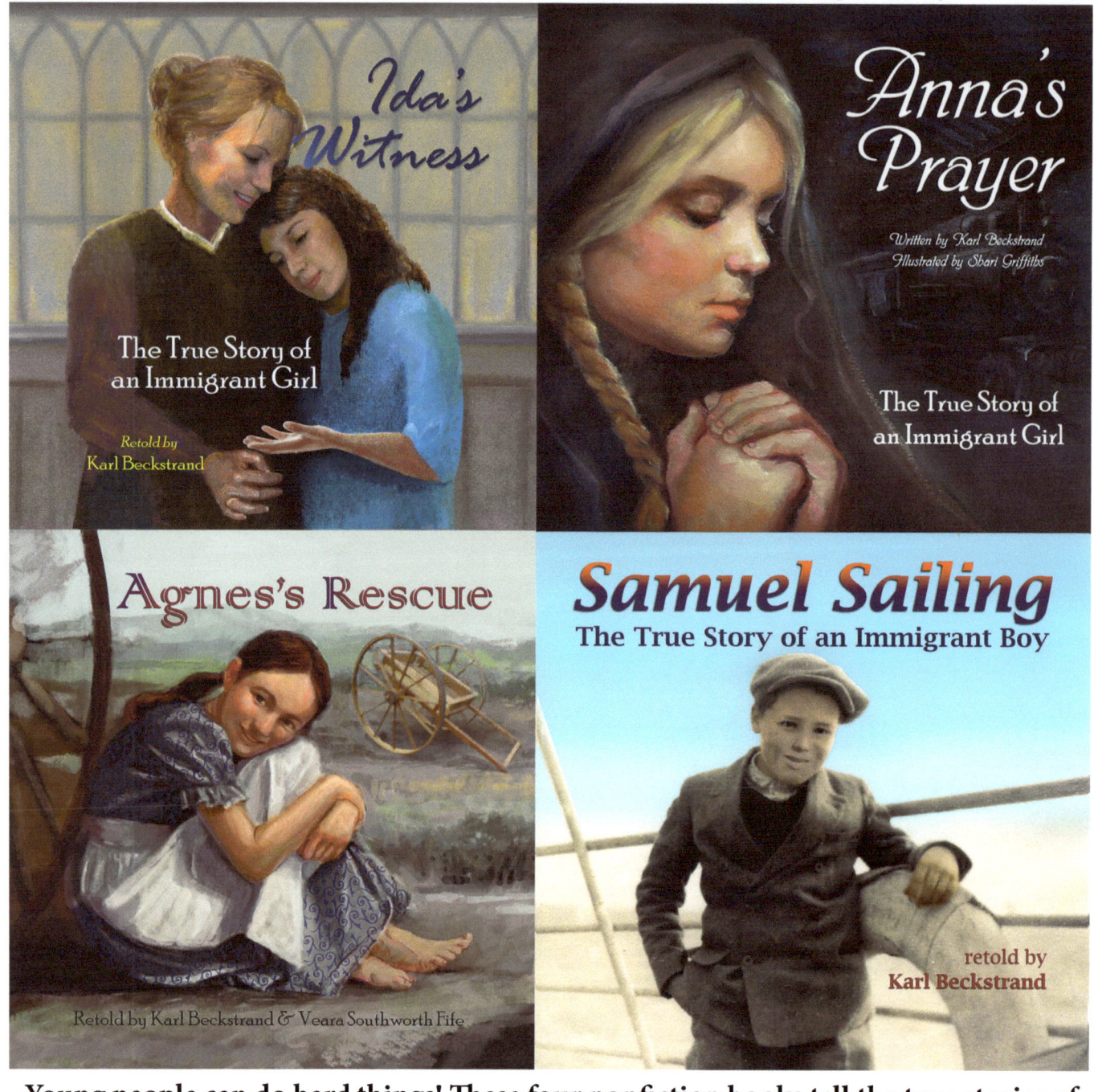

Young people can do hard things! These four nonfiction books tell the true stories of four children, each seeking a better life: *Agnes's Rescue* (Book I, Scotland/Ireland, 978-1951599119), *Ida's Witness* (Book II, Sweden, 978-0985398859), *Anna's Prayer* (Book III, Sweden, 978-0985398866), *Samuel Sailing* (Book IV, South Africa, 978-1951599126). All touch on a universal hunger—the yearning for a family and a place to call home. Standalone tales of courage and faith for all ages (4 years & up, hard/soft/ebook, 1,000 – 2,000 words each). Get all four in a bundle: KidsWorldBooks.com

(YA western survival/suspense novel) A tough young woman and a Latino drifter both search for missing family in a Nevada silver rush land scheme that leaves each unsure who to trust—and scrambling to stay alive (clean, ages 14+). Award winner comes with additional short story. 54,000 words, 200 pages, 5.25"x8"; ISBN: 978-0692407974, eISBN: 978-1311882387, Audio ISBN: 978-1667060699

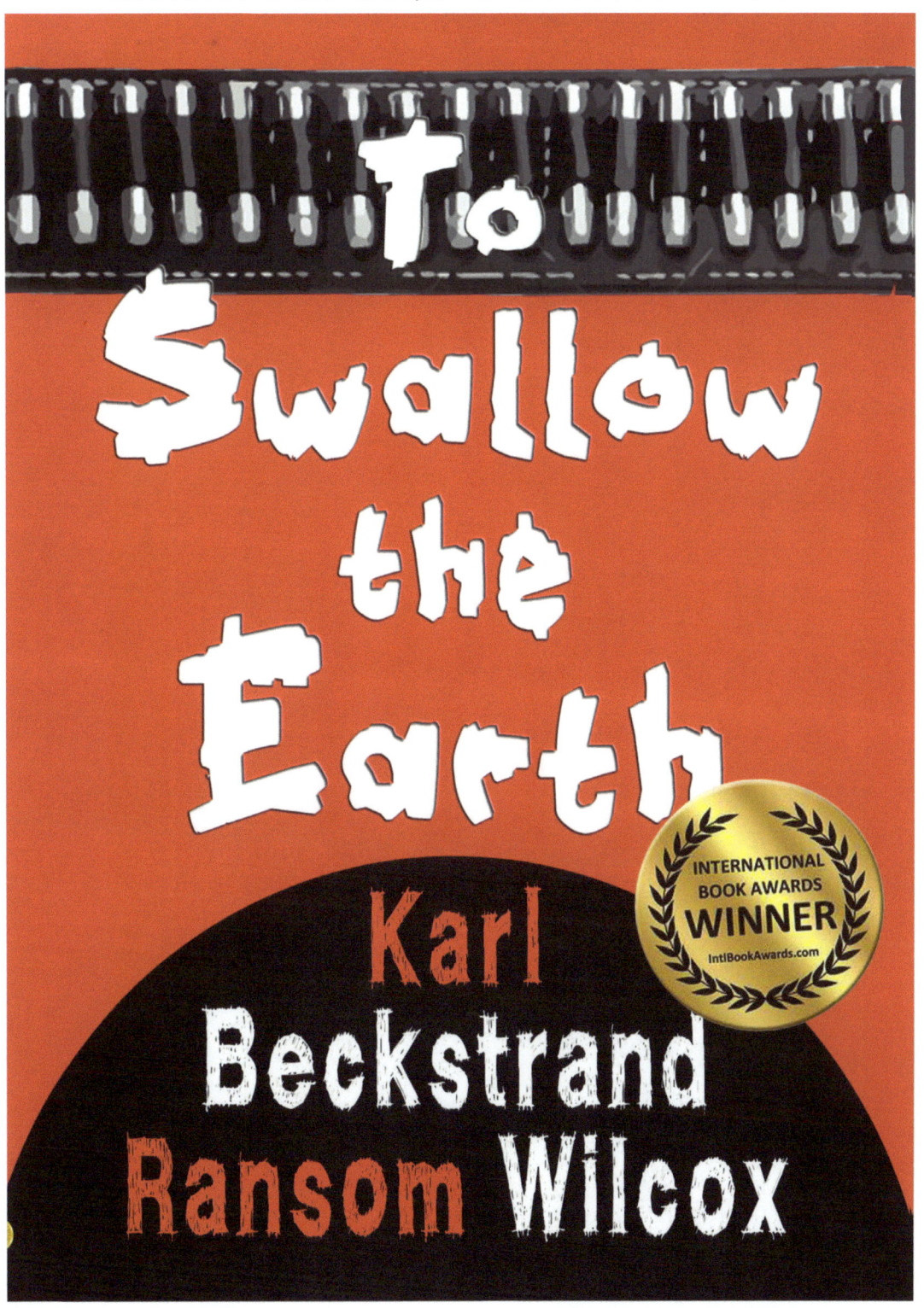

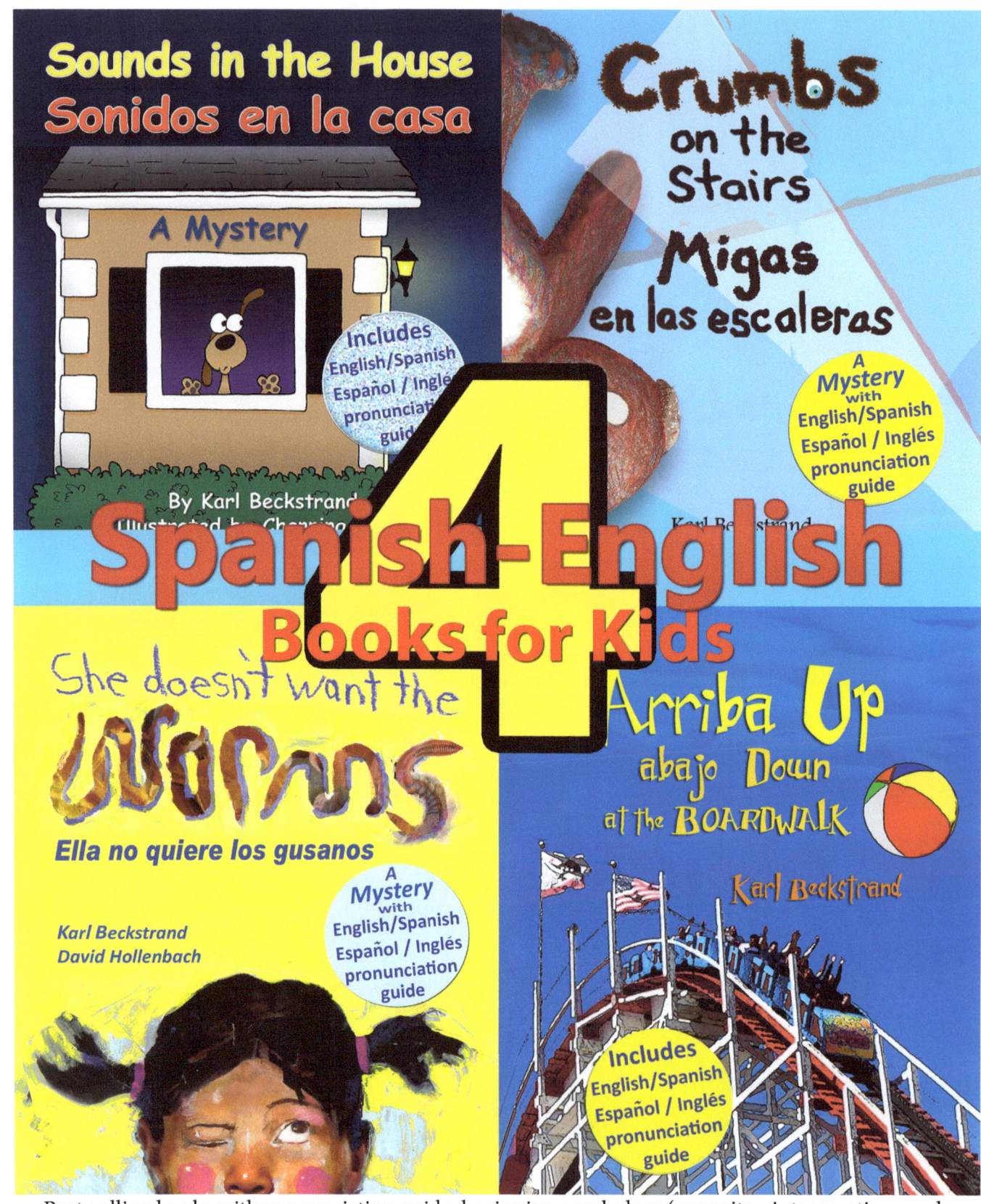

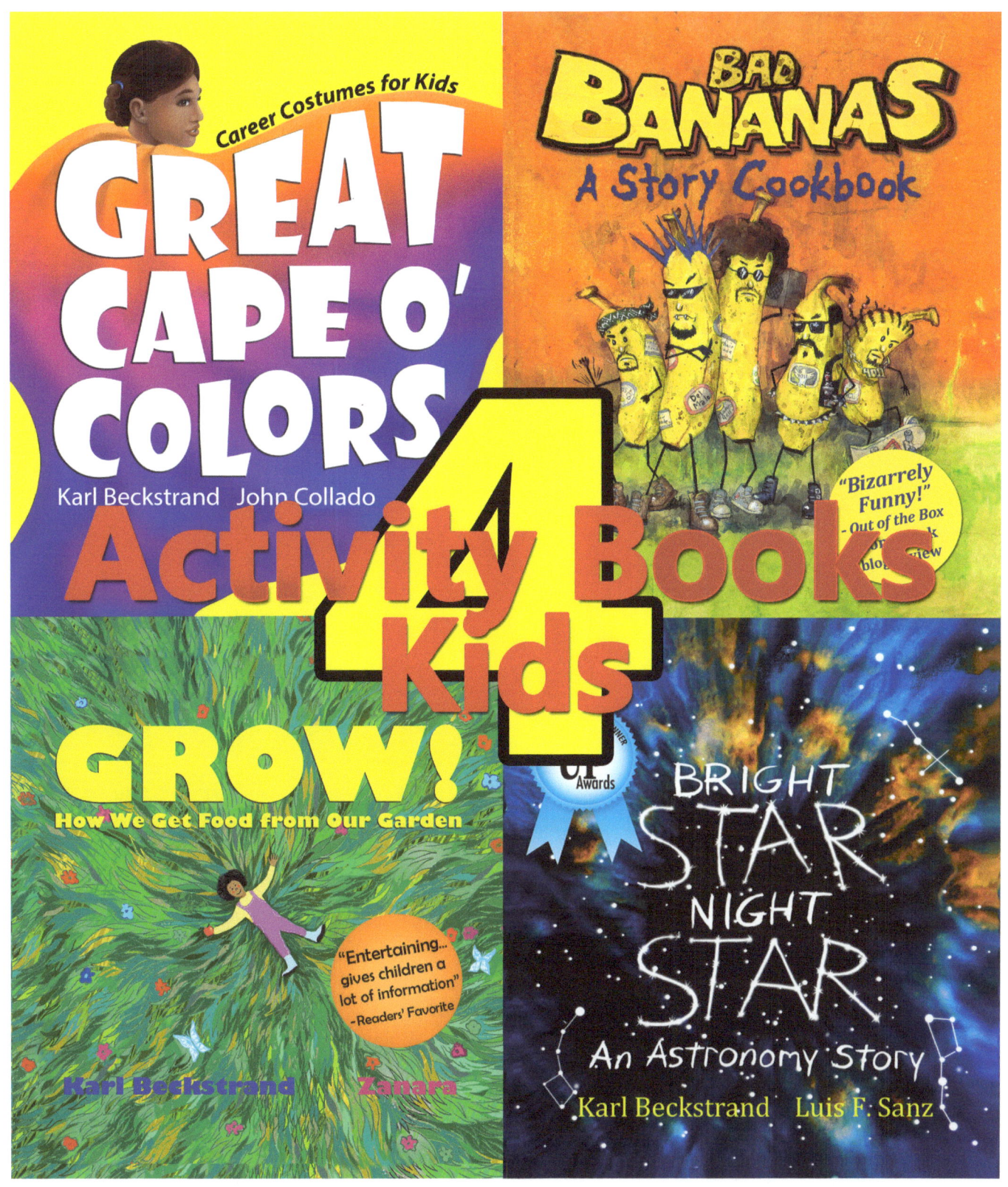

(Bound in one volume) Each story has educational activity, from trying on costumes to gardening to cooking to finding constellations (multiracial for ages 4 – 9 years, Pre-K – 5th grade; 110 pages; 1,150 words, soft ISBN: 979-8840381977

New

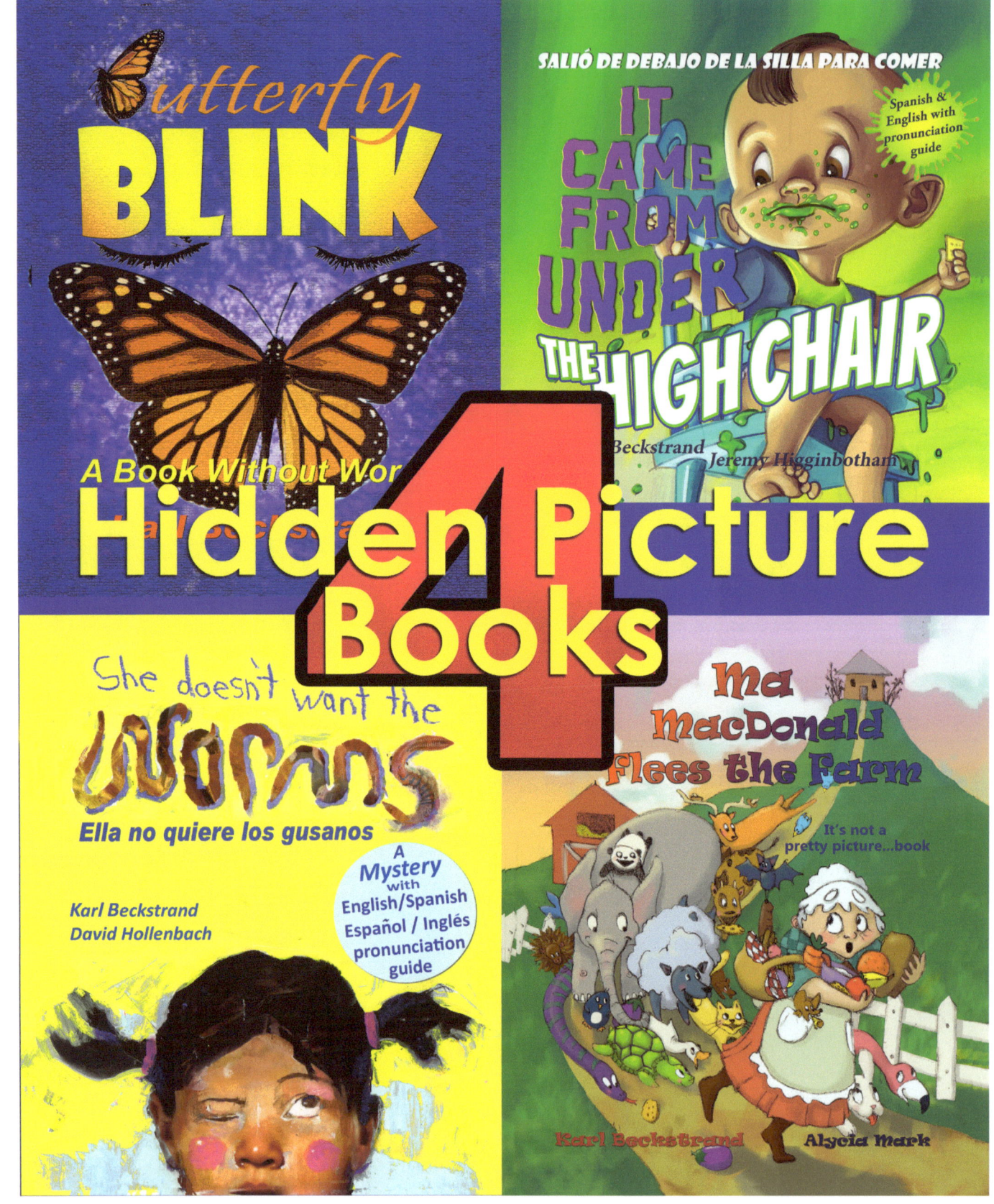

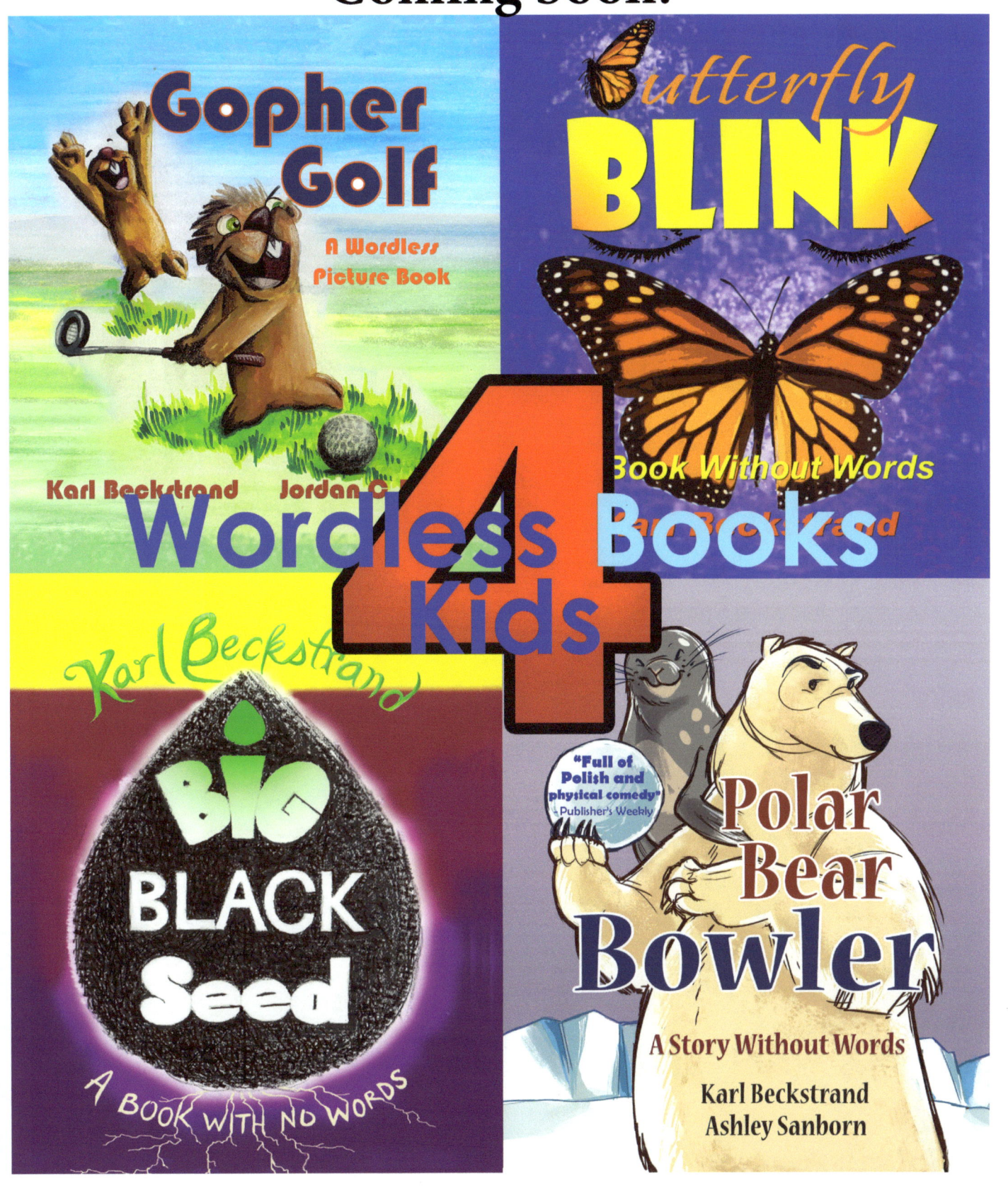

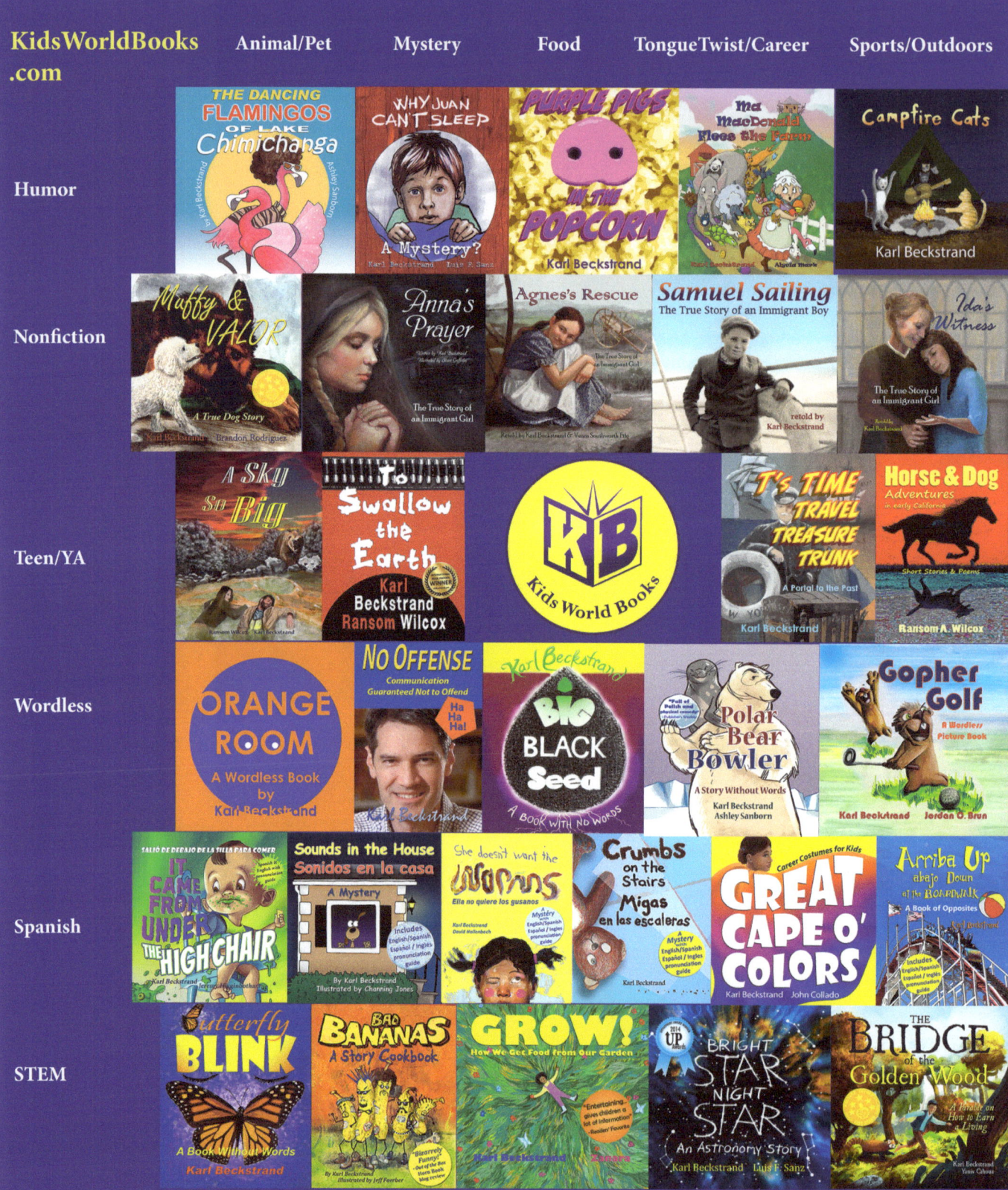

How many covers have circles on them? (Use QR code)

Two covers appear on the front, but not inside: *It Ain't Flat: A Memorizable Book of Countries* (request it at KidsWorldBooks.com) and *A Sky So Big: A Romantic Adventure* (978-0692426777, the romance version cover of *To Swallow the Earth*).

Premio Publishing has been delighting readers since 2004. Our award-winning YA fiction, self-help, ebook mysteries, nonfiction/biographies, Spanish language & bilingual picture books, short stories, clean romance, western, and STEM books feature many cultures. Nationally lauded (Publisher's Weekly, Kirkus, ForeWord Reviews, The Horn Book, School Library Journal), our titles have contributors of various ethnicities—and uplifting messages. Find our wholesome books via: Amazon/Kindle, Apple/iBooks, Árvore, Baker & Taylor, Barnes & Noble, Biblio, Brodart, EBSCO, Everand, Follett, Gardner's, Hertzberg/Perma-bound, Ingram, Kobo, Libraria, Library Direct, Mackin, MagicBlox, Mindworks, Odilo, OverDrive, Palace, Walmart.com, Target, and PremioPublishing.com. *See next page for prices and terms.*

College media instructor Karl W. Beckstrand is the best-selling author/illustrator of thirty multicultural/multilingual titles (60 ebooks—reviews by Publisher's Weekly, Kirkus, The Horn Book, and School Library Journal). Raised in San Jose, California, he has lived abroad, earned a B.A. in journalism, an M.A. in international relations & conflict resolution, and a broadcast & film certificate. He's won multiple publishing awards, including an International Book Award for his Y.A. western novel, To Swallow the Earth. Beckstrand loves volleyball and singing (in rock bands or choirs). His Y.A. stories, ebook mysteries, immigrant biographies, self-help, Spanish/bilingual, and STEM books feature ethnic characters—and usually end with a twist.

Other contributing artists: Channing Jones, David Hollenbach, Jeff Faerber, Luis F. Sanz, Shari Griffiths, Ash Rowan Nuccitelli Sanborn, Alycia Mark, Sean Sullivan, Brandon Rodriguez, John Collado, Yaniv Cahoua, Jeremy Higginbotham, Jordan C. Brun, Mike Condie, and Zanara

If you like our stories, please comment/rate online—and tell friends!
Other KidsWorldBooks bundles/compilations:

Trains Planes Trucks & Tubs
4 Stories of Immigrant Kids 978-1951599362
4 Food Books for Kids 978-1505693805
4 Funny Mysteries for Kids 978-1505690187
4 Spanish Books for Kids (single language) 978-1505671704
4 Spanish-English Books for Kids 978-0977606566
4 STEM Books for Kids 978-1951599195
4 Sports Books for Kids 978-1951599171
4 Hidden Picture Books for Kids 978-1951599133
4 Wild Animal Books for Kids 978-1951599300
4 Multicultural Bedtime Stories for Wide Awake Kids 978-1951599294
4 Career Books for Kids 978-1951599270
4 Tongue Twisters for Tykes 978-1951599287
Boats, Boards, Buggies & Bikes
Holiday Books for Kids

Fiction & nonfiction books in the works by Karl Beckstrand:
Westerns, short stories, self-help (relationships), biographies (hard/soft/ebook/audio)
Dog & Horse Adventures: Short Stories (sequel to *Horse & Dog*)
Rocket Kid on Planet Eyeball
Animal Submarine
Clatter, Shatter, Tatter, Splatter
Microscopic Minions
Animals in Black & White
This Pie is Mine
Me and the Sea

FREE multicultural ebooks, lesson plans, exclusive bundles & online SECRETS gratis:

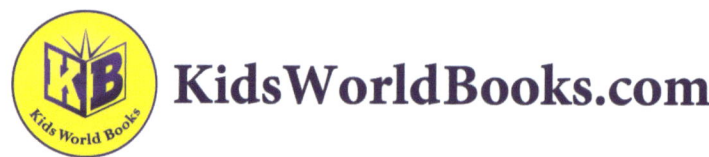

KidsWorldBooks.com

Retail prices/terms   School/library prices/terms

648 W. Wasatch St., Midvale, UT 84047 info@PremioBooks.com 801-953-3793

www.ingramcontent.com/pod-product-compliance
Lightning Source LLC
Chambersburg PA
CBHW040454220526
45473CB00004B/1632